TRAINING FOR THE MULTICULTURAL MANAGER

*A Practical and Cross-Cultural Approach
to the Management of People*

Pierre Casse

First Edition

SIETAR

The Society for Intercultural Education, Training and Research
Washington, DC

First Edition
July 1982

Copyright© 1982 by
Pierre Casse

Library of Congress Catalog Card Number: 82-060842
ISBN 0-933934-09-2

Manufactured in the United States of America

10 9 8 7 6 5 4 3 2

Dedicated to Dr. Diane L. Zeller, a friend and a pioneer in the Intercultural Field.

Table of Contents

Acknowledgments

The author wishes to express his gratitude for permission to use the following materials:

I. Briggs Meyer for the special material found on pages 57-8, from *Introduction to Type,* © 1976. Used with permission of Consulting Psychologists Press Inc.

The Coverdale Organization, Inc. for the use of "A Systematic Approach to Getting Things Done and Achieving Objectives," 1976. Found on pages 27-8.

F.E. Fiedler, M.M. Chemers and L. Mahar for the test found on pages 48-9, from *Improving Leadership Effectiveness*, page 8, published in New York by John Wiley and Sons, Inc. in 1976.

J. Daniel Hess, for the photograph on page 71, from *From the Other's Point of View,* published in Scottdale, PA by Herald Press in 1980.

Materials from *The Collected Works of C.G. Jung*, translated by R.F.C. Hull, Bollingen Series XX. Vol. 6: *Psychological Types* that were the basis for the self-assessment exercise on pages 38-40. Copyright © 1971 by Princeton University Press.

J.W. Humble, for his description of the factors that influence performance found on page 7, from *Management by Objectives in Banking*, page 31 (Ernest Sykes Lecture 1970). Published by The Institute of Bankers in London.

"Motivational Feedback Opinnionnaire," designed by D.F. Michalak and found on pages 72-3, from *The 1973 Annual Handbook for Group Facilitators,* pp. 44-45, edited by J.E. Jones and J.W. Pfeiffer. Used with permission of University Associates.

C.R. Mill and L. Porter for "Dilemmas of Leadership," found on pages 59-60, from *The Reading Book for Laboratories in Human Training*, page 40, copyright © 1972, NTL Institute. Reproduced by special permission.

"Yin/Yang: A Perspective of Theories of Group Development" by A.G. Banet, found on pages 133-4, from *The 1976 Annual Handbook for Group Facilitators,* pp. 176-77, edited by J.E. Jones and J.W. Pfeiffer. Used with permission of University Associates.

"The Maslow Need Hierarchy" by S.L. Pfeiffer, found on pages 103-5, from *The 1972 Annual Handbook for Group Facilitators,* pp. 125-129, edited by J.W. Pfeiffer and J.E. Jones. Used with permission of University Associates.

"The Allegory of the Man Who Walked on Water," found on pages xi-xii, from *Tales of the Dervishes* by Idries Shah, copyright © 1967. Reprinted by permission of E.P. Dutton, Inc.

The author also wishes to acknowledge with gratitude the photographs at the beginning of each workshop by M.L. Bussat and the editorial assistance of Darcy Fay, who saw this book to its completion.

Foreword

In his second book on cross-cultural training, Pierre Casse looks at management and managerial training from a cross-cultural perspective. From his point of view, management is polycentric, universal and multicultural.

He questions the notion that management is an American (US) invention. He suggests instead that management is an ancient art which has been with us for a very long time in many countries and cultures. Furthermore, he claims that the recognition of this fact depends on what we mean by management and how this concept is defined by peoples of different cultures. Actually, the ideas presented in the book may mean different things depending on our cultural perceptions.

He distinguishes between traditional management training and the demands which today's rapidly changing environment and complex organizational systems place on modern managers. According to him, managers are multicultural not only when they work with people from other countries but also with people from the same country, who speak the same language, have the same national heritage and yet, have different ways to look at the world. We each have our own separate realities, a world of our own construction defined by our own perceptions, beliefs, values and assumptions which form our unique, individual cultures. In this context, all managers are indeed multicultural.

Modern managers have been shifting from seeking solutions on a one-to-one basis to a more collective approach. They want to draw on the strengths and skills of their management teams towards the achievement of a common goal. It is their role to bring together into a viable team (culture), people with various backgrounds, personalities, experiences and training.

In motivating their people effectively, managers will profit from examining who they and their people are as individual cultures and how these affect their working relations. The workshops presented in this book will be valuable both to trainers and managers working from a cross-cultural perspective.

The workshops have been carefully designed using modern behavioral theories in a practical framework. All the exercises and cultural illustrations are task-related and use examples with which the experienced manager can readily identify. Both can be easily adapted to a variety of situations and used by personnel who do not have managerial duties.

I have seen Pierre Casse in action numerous times and have successfully applied some of his materials. When utilized judiciously, not as canned presentations, but as tools adjusted to the participants' cultures, they work and they work well!

This book, which is long overdue, fills a gap in the literature on crosscultural management training and constitutes a welcome aid for trainers and OD consultants.

> *Roxana Martin*
> *Personnel Officer, Staff Development*
> *and Training*
> *Pan American Health Organization*
> *Washington, DC*
> *June 1982*

Preface

The Allegory of the Man Who Walked on Water[1]

A conventionally minded dervish, from an austerely pious school, was walking one day along a river bank. He was absorbed in concentration on moralistic and scholastic problems, for this was the form which Sufi teaching had taken in the community to which he belonged. He equated emotional religion with the search for ultimate Truth.

Suddenly his thoughts were interrupted by a loud shout: someone was repeating the dervish call. "There is no point in that," he said to himself, "because the man is mispronouncing the syllables. Instead of intoning UA HU, he is saying U YA HU."

Then he realized that he had a duty, as a more careful student, to correct this unfortunate person, who might have no opportunity to be rightly guided, and was therefore probably only doing his best to attune himself to the idea behind the sounds.

So he hired a boat, and made his way to the island in midstream from which the sound appeared to come. There he found a man sitting in a reed hut, dressed in a dervish robe, moving in time to his own repetition of the initiatory phrase. "My friend," said the first dervish, "you are mispronouncing the phrase. It is incumbent on me to tell you this, because there is merit for him who gives and for him who takes advice. This is the way in which you speak it," and he told him.

"Thank you," said the other dervish humbly.

The first dervish entered his boat again, full of satisfaction at having done a good deed. After all, it was said that a man who could repeat the sacred formula correctly could even walk on the waves: something that he had never seen, but had always hoped—for some reason—to be able to achieve.

Now he could hear nothing from the reed hut, but he was sure that his lesson had been well taken. Then he heard a faltering U YA HU as the second dervish started to repeat the phrase in his old way.

While the first dervish was thinking about this, reflecting on the perversity of humanity and its persistence in error, he suddenly saw a strange sight. From this island, the other dervish was coming toward him walking on the surface of the water.

---

[1] From *Tales of the Dervishes* by Idries Shah. Copyright (c) 1967 by Idries Shah. Reprinted by permission of the publisher, E.P. Dutton, Inc.

Amazed, he stopped rowing. The second dervish walked up to him, and said, "Brother, I am sorry to trouble you, but I have come out to ask you again the standard method of making the repetition you were telling me, because I find it difficult to remember it."

Idries Shah
Tales of the Dervishes

Introduction to the Workshop Approach

"We have in modern life placed so much emphasis on what is logical and rational that we have become preoccupied with 'figuring out the right answer' in our heads rather than seeing, hearing and feeling what is really going on inside and around us, and responding to it according to its demands and according to what we have to do to meet our needs."

S. Herman

Who is the Multicultural Manager?

This book has been written for managers who have to deal with intercultural matters as well as for training specialists who prepare them for their very challenging tasks. It is based on two assumptions, namely that all managers are *multicultural* and that management training should be adjusted to *cross-cultural issues.*

The multicultural manager is someone who has to handle things, ideas and people belonging to different cultural environments. He or she can work either in a multinational corporation, an international organization, an institution located in a foreign country or even in local, regional or national organizations in which people do not share the same patterns of thinking, feeling and behaving.

In using this very wide definition of a multicultural manager, it is actually claimed that all managers within all organizations are multicultural. Some of them are maybe more involved in intercultural issues than others but all have to direct, assist and coach people with different cultural backgrounds characterized by various values, beliefs and assumptions.

Without realizing it, most managers have been multicultural in their jobs. So far there was not a pressing need for them to be aware of that fundamental dimension of their management of people (perceived in some cultures as "Resources"). This has been changed. Intuition alone is not enough any longer. More knowledge in the intercultural field is now required from the local, national and international managers.

Thus, traditional management training must be adjusted to the new requirements of the managerial functions. Management activities related to planning, organizing, leading and controlling have to be approached from a cross-cultural perspective if private and public organizations want to keep up their productivity (economic, social, *and* "cultural") inside and outside to the countries or cultures they belong.

The challenge for the intercultural trainer is to see how critical managerial processes such as communication, problem-solving, decision-making, performance appraisal, recruitment, promotions etc. can be (a) transplanted from one culture to another with the necessary adjustments and (b) presented to the managers of any kind of organization so that they can put their own actions into an intercultural perspective and learn from it.

Management is Multicultural!

In reading this book managers can expect to learn how to question some of their basic assumptions regarding the meaning of management, leadership, motivation, teamwork and participative management and then learn how to take full advantage of various ways of constructing the management of people's reality.

Trainers will have an opportunity to get enough training materials in terms of self-assessment exercises,[1] simulations, case studies, etc. to be in a position to design their own programs.

Quite a lot of training materials have been borrowed from the managerial field (including management training) and used in this book. The originality of the approach is that a systematic attempt has been made to present it from an intercultural perspective. One looks at the same thing but from a different, shall we say wider, angle.

Five training workshops are presented in the book. For each of them the reader will find (1) an introduction to the theme of the workshop; (2) a clarification of its aim; (3) a presentation of the objectives to be achieved; (4) a description of the process to be followed (not necessarily in the order presented in the text) or training exercises to be used with some comments about the reactions of the managers who have already participated in such workshops; (5) an estimate of the time required to run the sessions; (6) some theoretical inputs to explain some of the key points dealt with during the workshop; and (7) some references to handouts which can be distributed to participants for further explorations and readings for those interested in knowing more about the examined topics.

None of the suggested training instruments claims to be representative of ideal ways of handling cross-cultural managerial issues or prob-

---

[1]Many self-assessment exercises are proposed in the following workshops. They are *not* tests. The difference is fundamental. A test is supposed to tell the "truth" about oneself. A self-assessment exercise only provides some information to think about. It is a starter. It is entirely up to the individual who knows himself or herself to make a judgment upon the accuracy of the outcome of the exercise. He or she is the only judge!

lems. All exercises should be applied with caution and creativity. Think about the dervish story...

The five main themes which have been selected (the meaning of management, managerial styles, motivation across cultures, synergistic teamwork, and participative management) are presented with cultural illustrations from various parts of the world including North America, Latin America, Asia, Middle East, Africa, and Europe.

Managing Stereotypes

The illustrations are tentative and largely based on *stereotypes* or both oversimplified and overgeneralized views of the selected cultures. All of them should be used as elements of reflection rather than absolute explanations. They should lead to further explorations with the following premises in mind:

(1) Stereotypes are not dangerous as long as one knows that they are what they are and one is able to control them; (2) Each individual has his or her unique way of perceiving, discovering, and constructing activity (including management) and is therefore a culture in himself or herself.

Readers are asked to read the descriptions of the five workshops and actually practice the proposed exercises with a critical mind. To disagree is perfectly appropriate if not recommended. To enjoy the process is highly valued...It will, of course, depend on the reader's cultural background...

Finally it should be said that the approach used in the book is basic. It is "a practical and cross-cultural approach to the management of people." It aims at helping managers train themselves. Nothing more. Nothing less.

Pierre Casse
Washington, DC
March 1982

TRAINING FOR THE MULTICULTURAL MANAGER

A Practical and Cross-Cultural Approach to the Management of People

"Thus the sage knows without traveling;
He sees without looking;
He works without doing."

Tao Te Ching

Workshop 1
The Meaning of Management:
Is management North American?

1. Introduction: There is a myth around in the world and that is that management is North American. That is not true. Management has always existed in different cultural forms. Everything depends, of course, on what we mean by management. This is exactly the purpose of this first workshop, namely to examine what management means for different people with different cultural backgrounds.

The workshop will focus upon management as a technique as well as (at the other end of the cultural spectrum) a philosophy.

Basic cultural assumptions, values and beliefs or ways of thinking, feeling and behaving will be analyzed in relation to the organization of human affairs.

There is more than one way to "manage". There are many ways to look at what human beings and organizations do so that "things get done". The multicultural manager is certainly concerned with that issue.

2. Aim: To define management using various cultural approaches.

3. Objectives: The participants in the workshop will:

(a) define management from an intercultural standpoint (group discussion);

(b) analyze the North American way to approach management and match it with a British one (group discussion and conceptual framework: Input 1);

(c) contemplate the ancient Chinese definition of planning (group discussion);

(d) compare some of the key cultural traits of the North American and Japanese way to practice management (group discussion, exercise and conceptual framework: Input 2);

(e) examine some cultural assumptions typical of the North American and Latin American managerial realities (exercise and group discussion);

(f) see what some of the North American perceptions regarding the French reactions about management are (exercise and group discussion);

(g) experience some of the Arabic assumptions regarding management (case study).

4. Process:

Exercise A. Each participant writes a half-page "essay" on "What is a multicultural manager?" Next they share their impressions with another member of the group and finally with all the participants in the workshop.

Exercise B. The trainer asks the group members to meet in trios and analyze the following definition from an intercultural viewpoint (identification of the cultural assumptions which are included in the definition):

"Managing is getting things done through other people."

Questions: 1. getting? (meaning what?)
2. things? (what about ideas?)
3. done? (so only the result counts?)
4. through? (with? for?)
5. other people? (what about the manager himself or herself?)
6. what about another definition?

Exercise C. The Mackenzie model of the management process and the Humble description of the factors that influence performance are provided to the group (Figure 1 and Figure 2).

Figure 1. The Management Process[1]

---

[1]Inspired by A. Mackenzie, "The Management Process 3-D," *Harvard Business Review* (November - December 1969).

Figure 2. Management by Objectives[2]

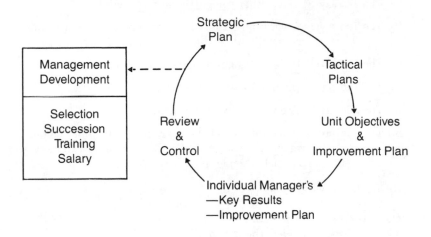

Exercise D. The group identifies and analyzes some of the key assumptions included in the following sentence:

"Don't just do something, stand there!"

Exercise E. All group members should read the 15 following statements which are borrowed from the *TAO*, a very old Chinese text on life and its meaning, and try to connect them with the meaning of management:[3]

1. The Tao says: All things go through their own transformation;

2. The Tao says: There are ways but the way is uncharted;

3. The Tao says: Be still while you work and keep full control over all;

4. The Tao says: Before and after are a sequence;

5. The Tao says: The way conforms to its own nature;

6. The Tao says: Truly, a cart is more than the sum of its parts;

7. The Tao says: The movement of the way is a return;

---

[2]J.W. Humble, *Management by Objectives in Banking* (London: The Institute of Bankers, 1970), p. 3.

[3]J. Friedman, *Retracking America: A Theory of Societal Planning* (New York: Doubleday, 1973), pp. 185-189.

8. The Tao says: The world may be known without leaving the house;

9. The Tao says: The farther you go, the less you will know;

10. The Tao says: Accordingly, the wise man knows without going, sees without seeing, does without doing.

11. The Tao says: By letting go, it all gets done;

12. The Tao says: Harmony experienced is known as constancy;

13. The Tao says: The world is won by refraining;

14. The Tao says: The strategists have a saying: "If I cannot be host, then let me be guest. But if it does not advance even an inch, then let me retire a foot";

15. The Tao says:

The Way eternal has no name.
A block of wood untooled, though small,
May still excel the world.
And if the king and nobles could
Retain its potency for good,
Then everything would freely give
Allegiance to their rule.

The earth and sky would then conspire
To bring the sweet dew down;
And evenly it would be given
To folk without constraining power.

Creatures came to be with order's birth,
And once they had appeared,
Came also knowledge of repose,
And with that was security.

In this world,
Compare those of the Way
To torrents that flow
Into river and sea.

第三十二章

道常無名樸雖小天下不敢臣侯王

若能守萬物將自賓天地相合以降

甘露民莫之令而自均始制有名名

亦既有夫亦將知止知止所以不殆。

譬道之在天下猶川谷之於江海也。

Participants use the matrix presented in Figure 3 and pinpoint:

1. Things that they found easy to understand;

2. Ideas they do not understand;

3. Comments they disagree with.

Figure 3. The Meaning of Planning: A Tao Perspective

1. Things I find *easy to understand.*	
2. Ideas I do *not understand.*	
3. Statements I *disagree with.*	

When the matrix is completed, the participants meet in pairs and try to help each other become more aware of their cultural reactions triggered by the "esoteric" text. They read their respective comments and then raise the following issues:

1. Why don't you understand? What is unclear to you? If you had to reformulate the statements what would you say? Why is it clear? Why do you disagree?

2. What is cultural in your reactions?

Exercise F. Five cultural assumptions related to the North American and Japanese cultures are presented to the group (Figure 4).

Figure 4. Contrasting Assumptions Between the North American and Japanese Cultures

NORTH AMERICAN	JAPANESE
• IMPATIENT	• PATIENT
• INFORMAL	• FORMAL
• ACTION ORIENTED	• AFFILIATION ORIENTED
• INDIVIDUALISTIC	• SOCIALISTIC
• CONCERNED WITH SUCCESS	• CONCERNED WITH LOSING FACE

After having discussed and clarified the above contrasting assumptions (participants are asked to document the 10 items), the group is split into two sub-groups, one representing the North American culture and the other Japanese culture. Each sub-group must guess using the five listed assumptions how managers from the culture they have been assigned would rate the organizational norms presented in the following chart:

Figure 5. Organizational Norms

Organizational Norms	Healthy	Unhealthy	Neutral	Not Relevant
1. Promotions will come if you wait.				
2. Be creative on-the-job.				
3. Self-development is encouraged.				
4. Do not compete with your colleagues.				
5. Overtime work is highly valued.				
6. Wear proper dress in office.				
7. Do not rock the boat.				
8. Obey orders.				
9. Follow procedures.				
10. Talk about your personal life.				

When they are ready, the two sub-groups compare their ratings and discuss them (justification of the similarities and the differences).

Exercise G. Participants receive the following instructions:

"Look at the picture hereunder and use your imagination to describe three conversations: (a) one typical of the North American culture; (b) the other typical of the Latin American culture, and finally; (c) one conversation between a North American and a Latin American. Do not be afraid of using stereotypes."

When they have finished, they meet in trios and analyze their respective dialogues trying to spot as many cultural traits and stereotypes of the North American and Latin American cultures as possible.

*D.A. Kolb, I.M. Rubin, and J.M. McIntyre, *Organizational Psychology (An Experiential Approach)* (Englewood Cliffs, NJ: Prentice Hall, Inc., 1971), p. 56.

Another way to proceed with this exercise is to show the picture and provide the three following conversations to the participants who meet in trios and analyze each one of them using the instructions on the right side of the page (10 minutes are used for each conversation):[4]

(1) NORTH AMERICAN CONVERSATION

(2) LATIN AMERICAN CONVERSATION

(3) LATIN AMERICAN AND NORTH AMERICAN CONVERSATION.

(See the Attribution Exercise pages 14-16).

---

[4]Created by John Schaeffer, Washington, DC

THE ATTRIBUTION EXERCISE

1. North American conversation:

"I'll tell you, Bob, that's where I like to put my money. The stock market has been wild lately. Can't make money any easier. You should participate in it more. Investments are everything."

"I know, Dad…but lately time has been hard to come by. Things have really kept me busy down at the office, but it should get easier when I become a full partner in the firm."

"Remember, it's going to cost you plenty to put those kids through school. And prices aren't getting any better. One can never have enough. Let me get in touch with my broker to see what he might be able to put together."

"I would appreciate that. Have him send any ideas to my office. Now, I'm off to the club for a game of squash. Have to go, mustn't be late. We'll talk later."

"Don't procrastinate on my advice. Act now if you possibly can. You'll be better off for it in the future."

"OK Dad. See you next week sometime."

"Look for values, beliefs, assumptions which underlie what the characters say."

ATTRIBUTIONS

ATTRIBUTIONS

2. Latin American conversation:

"Carlos, this sounds very unfortunate. It's truly hard to believe that she would refuse your proposal of marriage. What can she be thinking?"

"Uncle Roberto, I don't know...but I will try again. There is no other woman for me, she must be mine! But for now, I will let the matter rest for a short time."

"No, Carlos, you must not wait. She must be only testing you. Women are always playing these games. She loves you. But first, let me have a coffee with her father. We are old friends."

"You are right, Uncle. And there is no better wife for me in this city. She is beautiful, faithful, and comes from a good family. Everyone would do well by our marriage."

"And think of the healthy sons she could give you to carry on for us all, we can't forget that," joked Uncle Roberto. "Let's go for a pastry and discuss this matter some more."

"Certainly, Uncle, let's go."

ATTRIBUTIONS

3. Latin American and North American conversation:

"There is just no other way Jim, unless you want to give it up. In order to do business in Colombia, you must adapt yourself to our way of doing things. Many have ended in failure for not doing so."

"I do understand some of the differences, but why is it that *I* am forced to do all the changing? Who is the boss here? Do they not understand that my way has been very effective. They must be unconscious."

"Jim, of course you are the boss and your ways of managing are the best in the world, but they must be successfully adapted to our culture. For example, try paying more attention to your employees. If they like you, they will pay more attention to your desires and requests of them."

"Oh, what a bore that would be! They should work for me because I pay them to. All I ask for is eight hours of work per day. I have other things to do in my spare time. Why should I patronize my own employees? I have no time for the problems they bring to work with them. They work, I pay. What more? I don't want to hear about the sick relatives and the like."

"No, Jim, that attitude will never do. It sounds frightfully impersonal and will bring you problems. May I suggest that you try to be more flexible and reconsider this matter? There really is no way of avoiding this issue. You must face it successfully."

"What a mistake it was to locate a plant here just for the initial tax breaks. Little did I know what nonsense awaited me."

Exercise H. A list of 10 North American perceptions of the French regarding management is given to the group which has to decide if they are pre-conceived ideas or accurate identification of what French managers think, believe and do. (Participants put a check in the corresponding box—see Figure 6. Thirty minutes is devoted to this exercise.)

Figure 6. North American Perspectives

NORTH AMERICAN PERSPECTIVES	TRUE	FALSE	PARTLY TRUE & PARTLY FALSE
French Managers have a tendency to:			
1. Rely on improvisation when in doubt.			
2. Be sensitive to foreign interventions in their internal affairs.			
3. Be conservative.			
4. Be obsessed with institutions.			
5. Be very logical when reasoning.			
6. Look at the big picture and forget the details.			
7. Enjoy the stimulation from the exchange of abstract ideas.			
8. Be hierarchical.			
9. Be bureaucratic.			
10. Question what's not French.			

Afterwards, the group should compare their answers with the reactions of a French group of managers who went through the same exercise (see chart next page).

NORTH AMERICAN PERSPECTIVES	TRUE	FALSE	PARTLY TRUE & PARTLY FALSE
French Managers have a tendency to:			
1. Rely on improvisation when in doubt.			✔
2. Be sensitive to foreign interventions in their internal affairs.	✔		
3. Be conservative.		✔	
4. Be obsessed with institutions.			✔
5. Be very logical when reasoning.	✔		
6. Look at the big picture and forget the details.			✔
7. Enjoy the stimulation from the exchange of abstract ideas.	✔		
8. Be hierarchical.			✔
9. Be bureaucratic.		✔	
10. Question what's not French.		✔	

Exercise I. The group works on the "JONGLEI CANAL PROJECT" case study. (Part I only)[5]

Phase 1. 45 minutes, individual work (Participants read part I of the case and answer the two questions on page 22);

Phase 2. 60 minutes, team work (sharing ideas about the situation and on how to handle it);

Phase 3. 60 minutes, discussion in a plenary session (comparing the team locations);

Phase 4. 30 minutes, analysis of Part II of the case study in teams (comparing the outcome of the plenary session with what actually happened).

---

[5]Part II is only distributed at the beginning of Phase 4.

THE JONGLEI CANAL PROJECT
A CASE STUDY[6]

PART I

The Sudan, with an area of one million square miles, and with 200,000,000 acres of arable land, represents the largest country and the one richest in agricultural potential in Africa. It is thus often described as the bread-basket of the Arab World. Also with Libya, Egypt and Saudi Arabia on its northwestern, northern and eastern boundaries, respectively, and with Ethiopia, Kenya, Uganda, the Congo, Central African Republic and Chad on its southeastern, southern and western borders, the Sudan is described, and rightly so, as the "crossroads of African and Arab cultures".

Cross-cultural interaction of Arab and African peoples and cultures have been reflected in the internal make-up and composition of the Sudanese people. Northern Sudan, comprising two-thirds of the country's area and three-quarters of its population, i.e. twelve million people, has the greater part of the country's lands cultivable by irrigation or rainfall. It is also predominantly Arab and Muslim in culture, ethnic origin, religion, and social and political inclinations. The South, on the other hand, being largely hilly, and occupied with large expanses of forests and swampy areas (it is called Sud Region), is relatively poor and underdeveloped when compared to the North, which is economically and socially more developed.

The differences in economic and social development, and the disparities in cultural and ethnic origins between the North and the South have evolved into deeply held suspicion and mistrust that erupted into a civil war at the time of independence from the British and lasted for fifteen years. The religious and cultural overtones of the war have elicited the support of the neighboring countries to one side or the other; the African countries sided with the South and the Arab countries with the North. As the war took place in the South, it resulted in a lot of physical and social destruction. Grave damage was also done to faith, trust and confidence between the two parts of the country.

At the end of the war in 1971, one of the major concerns and priorities of the National government has been reconstruction, resettlement, and

---

[6]This case was prepared at the request of the World Bank by M. Hammour and Professor R. Nath from the public data available on the project as a basis for group discussion. (Cases are not designed to present illustrations of either correct or incorrect handling of administrative situations.) Neither the writers, the World Bank or the Sudanese Government are in any way accountable for the facts presented in the case.

rehabilitation of those who lost their homes and families. The new construction therefore provided for the establishment of a Regional government for the South. The Regional government comprises a High Executive Council and a People's Assembly. The High Executive Council is responsible for general administration and implementation of the development projects. The People's Assembly is charged with the duties of developing legislation for the South.

The Regional government, headed by a Deputy President, is a microcosm of the National government. Except for the Ministries of Defense and Foreign Affairs, each Ministry in the North had its counterpart in the South. Ministers in the South have had the same status and prestige as their counterparts in the North. Moreover, the structure, functions, and terms of reference of the Ministries in the North and the South are primarily the same.

One of the major development projects undertaken by the National government in Khartoum has been the Jonglei Canal, which was intended, in addition to developmental purposes, to drain the swamp area in the Sud Region and carry the water to the Nile, thereby helping to solve the projected irrigation water deficits of Sudan and Egypt in the 1980's. Without the Canal Project, this deficit would amount to over six million cubic meters. The construction of the canal would start from the right bank of the White Nile at Jonglei village, shortly after the Nile enters the Sudan. The canal would run almost straight north to the mouth of the river Sobat (a tributary of the Nile) near Malakal, a distance of about 300 km; it would have a capacity of 20 million cubic meters per day; and would deliver 4 million cubic meters of additional water at Malakal. Half of this additional water would be available to the Sudan, the other half to Egypt. Each country would be responsible for 50% of the financing, the total of which has been estimated at LS. 70 million, or about $200 million.

The administrative vehicle for designing the project proposal was a Joint Commission consisting of representatives from irrigation ministries of the two countries.

The Joint Commission conducted several feasibility studies. The technical feasibility study found that there were no major technical problems in implementing the project and all the technical work required can be carried out by Sudanese and Egyptian experts without any foreign assistance. The financial feasibility study indicated that the project is economically viable, although there would be a need for securing funds from foreign sources.

Cost-benefit analysis indicated that the benefits to be derived from the project would far outweigh the costs involved. These benefits would include:

1. Provision of increased irrigation in both Sudan and Egypt. It would thereby open avenues for development of the inhabitants of the Sudanese territory who are currently living under primitive conditions. The introduction of agriculture to this primitive area would not only raise the living standards but also would put local inhabitants in touch with agricultural markets in the north.

2. Relief from the annual devastating effects of the floods.

3. Improved navigation along the Nile.

4. Reclamation of approximately 200,000 acres for cultivation of new cash crops, mainly rice.

5. Improvement in health conditions of the region.

In the long run, agricultural development and health improvement should lead to a better standard of living.

The Joint Commission submitted its recommendations to the Council of Ministers of the National Government of Sudan who wholeheartedly endorsed the project in 1975. A favorable decision was also rendered by the Egyptian government. As a result, the Council of Ministers appointed a managing director at the rank of Deputy Minister who reported directly to the Council. Reporting to the managing director were financial, administrative, and engineering assistants. A resident engineer located at the site also reported directly to the managing director. The organization set-up of the project is shown in the organization chart below.

Figure 7. Project Organization

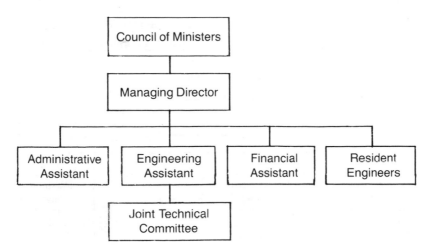

As can be seen from the chart, there is a Joint Technical Committee that reports to the engineering assistant. This committee consists of technical experts from both Sudan and Egypt. The first managing director was an undersecretary of the Ministry of Irrigation which had taken a lead role in the initiation of the project. Since the project had a national visibility and was of major national significance, several ministries indicated a desire to participate in the project. However, these requests were ignored by the managing director because he feared that this would greatly increase the size of the project organization resulting in a lot of red tape, decreased efficiency and unnecessary time delays.

Soon after the foreign financing was cleared, the managing director dispatched a team of technical experts to the site. When these experts arrived at the site, demonstrations against the project erupted all over the Jonglei area. In addition, political demonstrations were held in the South against the project. These demonstrations continued with full force through the latter part of 1975. Any attempt to stop these demonstrations only led to further protests.

In 1976, the Council of Ministers met again with the managing director to consider the tense situation that was created by the riots and demonstrations. It became obvious to the council that a well-thought-out plan of action had to be executed in order to save the situation.

Your Task:

The Council of Ministers has invited you as an outside organizational consultant. Please submit to the Council your plan of action, which should include:

(a) Your diagnosis of the situation, particularly what went wrong and why.

(b) Your recommendations as to how to handle the overall situation.

Jonglei Canal Project — Structural Chart

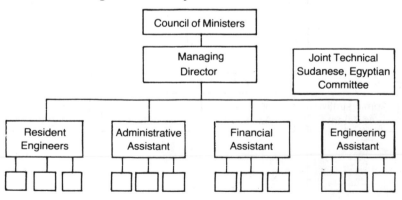

PART II

Measures Taken by the Central Government
to Remedy the Situation

The government formed a high-level Inquiry Commission. Its membership included a wide cross-section of specialists - Southerners, both intellectuals and politicians. Concerned ministries and departments have also been included in the Commission, such as the Ministries of Health, Social Affairs, Cooperatives and Information. After three months of study and investigative work, the Commission submitted its report. Its findings included the direct and indirect reasons that led to the political unrest and to the apprehension entertained by the Southerners regarding Jonglei. Its recommendations included the steps it perceived as necessary in order to repair the damage that was done, and to allay the fears and the suspicions voiced during the disturbances.

After a series of studies and probing between the Central government and the Regional government, the report was adopted as an Action Program, and the Inquiry Commission was assigned the task of implementing its report and became the Project Commission. The Managing Director was confirmed as the Chairman of the new Project Commission. The work of the Commission has been conducted very smoothly and effectively ever since, and the coordination, collaboration, and interaction required between the different parties involved at the central, regional, and local levels have been carried out efficiently and in the best spirit and understanding. The involvement and participation of the local people and the concern about the success and completion of the project has been so noticeable, that it has been predicted that the project might be completed before the target date previously set.

The Commission's Report:

Reasons behind the disturbances:

1. The Central Government and the Project Committee have put too much emphasis on technical and economic considerations at the expense of social and ecological considerations.

2. The Project Commission and the Ministry of Irrigation have inadvertently played down the role of coordination and functional relations required between them and other ministries and departments involved in the Project's execution, especially the Regional Ministry of the South. However, the report elaborates on the importance of this process of coordination, collaboration, and interaction in the following ways:

(a) The Ministry of Social Affairs and Community Development should study and assess ways of living, social and cultural values, attitude towards change, and beliefs and aspirations of the people of the Sud Region.

(b) The Ministry of Information should disseminate information and data germane to the Project's benefits accruing to the people. It should also relay to the Central and Regional governments any misgivings or erroneous ideas related to the Project, as well as any mythical apprehensions or superstitious values expressed or implied by the people against change or development.

(c) The Ministries of Agriculture and Cooperatives had the potential to help in devising new ways and means of introducing agriculture, developing cattle rearing and fishing, without seriously destroying or jeopardizing the traditional modes of living of the local people.

3. People, who were living in the area and expected to be affected most by the Jonglei Project, were left completely out of the picture. Hence, all their information about the project came from elements hostile to the project and to the North-South rapprochement. Moreover, people's nostalgic attachments to their old ways of living, mainly hunting, fishing and cattle-rearing, compounded their fears.

The Commission's Recommendations

1. Implementation of the project should not be assigned to a single individual and a traditional organization. It should rather be given to a task force that represents all the concerned Ministries, specialized people, and Southerners in their capacity as the directly interested group. The Managing Director should be appointed and regarded as one among equals who works in consultation and cooperation with other parties involved.

2. The Task Force would reserve the right to appoint as many subcommittees as possible and to draft into these subcommittees any individuals or groups that could contribute towards a viable and constructive formula that would bail out the project and at the same time satisfy the people in the area.

3. Advance study groups in areas of sociology and information systems should go to the area, study and assess the situation, and regularly brief the Central and Regional governments on the ecology and views of the people in the area regarding the project.

4. A joint committee of Southern politicians, local leaders, Northern politicians and professionals and technicians should start a campaign of exploring the facts and correcting any misunderstanding that might have been created.

5. A system of regular meetings between all parties involved, i.e. the Central government, the Regional government, the Managing Director and his Task Force, and the subcommittees, in addition to local leaders, should be established. Such meetings should assess progress, investigate areas of discontent and frustration, and suggest more viable methods of operations and interaction.

6. Since the local people's socio-emotional commitment to their existing style of life is forthright and conspicuous, the commission has suggested that any developmental endeavors should be directed towards rendering their traditional ways and means of living more efficacious, more modern, and more rewarding. Any intended large-scale or radical transformation in their economic or social well-being, such as the introduction of rice plantation, should be long-term and on a phased basis.

7. Relations and interactions between technical, administrative, political, and social factors involved in the implementation of this project should be clearly delineated and effectively brought home to all those involved in the planning or implementation of this project. This represents an extremely important point that would be conducive to a comprehensive and integrated teamwork approach. It is also important for a thorough and multidisciplinary probing and handling of the problems of the project.

5. Time: One full day.

6. Conceptual Framework: To be used by the trainer during or after the workshop to clarify some of the identified issues.

INPUT 1

(A) The Management Process:
The North American Approach[7]

("Getting Things Done Through Other People")

Management Phase	**Define and Establish**
Strategic Planning	1. Mission - what business are we in?
	2. Philosophy - what kind of life do we want to live?

---

[7]Designed by M. Robert Youker, Economic Development Institute of the World Bank.

	3. Long Range Objectives and Goals
	4. Problems and Opportunities - in external and internal environment
	5. Overall Strategy - basic approach
	6. Major Program Areas
Multi-Year Programming	7. Five Year Program Objectives and Goals
	8. Program Strategies for Meeting Goals
	9. Financial Plans
	10. Organizational Structure
	11. Policies and Procedures
	12. Program Plans (five years)
Operational Planning	13. Budget Objectives (one year)
	14. Budgets
	15. Detailed Action Plans (MBO)
	16. Schedules (calendar dates)
	17. Resources, Staffing, and Training
Leadership and Motivation	18. Responsibilities of Staff
	19. Communication of Objectives
	20. Coordination of Effort
	21. Standards of Performance
Implementation and Control	22. Reporting Systems
	23. Analysis and Measurement of Performance
	24. Corrective Action
	25. Changes in Objectives and Plans

(B) The Management Process: A British Approach

"The Coverdale Approach to Management"[8]

Figure 8. A Systematic Approach to Getting Things Done and Achieving Objectives

INSTRUCTION OR STIMULUS TO DO SOMETHING ▶ **AIMS** ▼

- CONSIDERING FOR WHAT PURPOSE/S THE JOB IS BEING TACKLED
- SPECIFYING WHAT WE WANT TO ACHIEVE – TO END UP WITH
- SETTING STANDARDS BY WHICH TO MEASURE OUR ACHIEVEMENT

INFORMATION	GATHERING RELEVANT KNOWLEDGE, EXPERIENCE, IDEAS, EVIDENCE ETC. ASSESSING THE RISKS INVOLVED.
WHAT HAS TO BE DONE (W.H.T.B.D.)	HAVING LOOKED AT ALL THE INFORMATION, STATING THOSE THINGS THAT NEED TO BE DONE NEXT.
PLANNING	SPECIFYING IN DETAIL HOW THINGS WILL BE DONE . . . . WHO DOES WHAT, WHEN, WHERE, HOW.
ACTION	**CARRYING OUT THE PLAN**
REVIEW	CHECKING TO SEE IF PROGRESS HAS BEEN MADE TOWARDS AIMS . . . . CONSIDERING WHAT WENT WELL . . . . WHAT DIFFICULTIES OCCURRED . . . . LEADING TO . . . . **PLANNING TO IMPROVE NEXT TIME**

Figure 9. The Coverdale Process

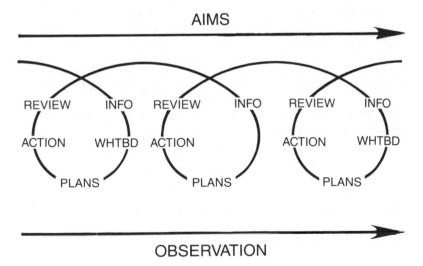

[8]Developed by the Coverdale Organization, copyright (c) 1976.

The Coverdale approach explores and contrasts the static, mechanistic, organic and ethical systems which operate in any organization. The principles and practices derived from mechanistic or static systems should not be directly applied to organic systems. Different emphases on the use of thought and action are appropriate according to each occasion. Moreover, the approach to a particular situation will be conditioned by the degree to which it is open or closed. Judgment of the requisite form of approach will be a function of an individual's awareness of the total situation.

Coverdale observed and systematized the balance of thought with action that people tend to use naturally in getting things done. These stages - purpose objectives and success criteria, information, stating what has to be done, plans, action, and review to improve - constitute a 'Systematic Approach' which can be a useful aid for thinking, in a number of ways. The individual may consciously use this as a means of self-discipline, ensuring that action follows preparation and that a subsequent review will give feedback and feed-forward to enable a closer movement towards declared goals with each effort. In a team the Systematic Approach can also be used to coordinate the thinking skills of its members so that each judges the contribution that is appropriate at a given time. This leads to a concerted effort and awareness of common purpose. Again in the team context, it can be used as a model for appropriate delegation.

At the Organizational level, the stages of thought can be useful as a framework for looking at the organization. It then becomes apparent that different stages and styles of thinking are desirable at different levels, e.g. at the Director level the primary need is for skill in setting direction, establishing success criteria and ensuring that the next level's policies are developed. At General Management level the crucial thinking lies in the area of setting policy, defining and delegating achievable objectives. At lower levels the skills required move through acquiring and using information to set more specific objectives, identifying what has to be done, and taking the risk of getting into action. In staff departments, personnel operate from the review stage and need to be competent both at analyzing and at feeding back information which will be used.

Coverdale draws on a philosophy which stresses an individual's desire to be of value to fellow human beings and the potential of the individual for achievement in the future.

INPUT 2

North American and Japanese Assumptions Regarding Management[9]

North American	Japanese
1. Short-term employment	1. Life-time employment
2. Rapid evaluations and promotions	2. Slow evaluation and promotions
3. Specialized careers	3. Non-specialized careers
4. Individual decisions	4. Consensual decision-making
5. Individual responsibility	5. Collective responsibility
6. Explicit, formal control	6. Implicit, informal control
7. Segmented concern about people	7. Holistic concern about people

7. Handouts and Readings:[10]

(a) Handouts

Alromaithy A., and Reynolds A., "A New Model for International Training," *Training and Development Journal,*" October 1981, pp. 63-69.

Attwood, T.J., "Greater Cross-cultural Sensitivity Needed in International Operations," *AMA International Forum*, Vol. 67., No. 7, July 1978, pp. 23-31.

Batdorf L.L., "Cultural Sensitivity Training," *Training and Development Journal,* August 1980, pp. 28-40.

Bass, B.M., and Thiagarajan, K.M., "Preparing Managers for Work in Other Countries," *European Training,* (Bradfort), 1 (2), Summer 1972, pp. 117-132.

Chowdhry, K., "Developing Administration for Tomorrow," *Indian Journal of Public Administration,* New Delhi 15(2), April-June 1969, pp. 221-227.

Crapo R., "T, D and Z," *Training and Development Journal,* October 1981, pp. 102-110.

---

[9]From the film by W.G. Ouchi, "Type Z: An Alternative Management Style" (Chrysler Learning, Inc., 1979).

[10]Trainers may select the handouts and readings to be used in the workshop among the documents hereunder.

Crockett, W.J., "Our Two Worlds," *Training and Development Journal,*" May 1982, pp. 60-68.

De Bettignies, H.C., Rhinesmith, S.H., "Developing the International Executive," *European Business,* Paris (24), January 1970, pp. 52-57.

Dernegi, T.I., "Turkish Management Survey," Istanbul, Turkish Management Association, April 1965.

Endicott, C., Lindheim Markey, T., and Slocomb, N.A., "Assignment USA," *The Bridge,* Fall 1981.

Gibney, F., "The Japanese and Their Language," *Encounter,* March 1975, p. 33.

Gordon, B.K., "Japan, the United States, and Southeast Asia," *Harvard Business Review,* March-April 1971.

Hall, J., "What Makes a Manager Good, Bad, or Average," *Psychology Today,* August 1976, p. 52.

Harris, P.R., "Managing Cultural Differences," *The Bridge,* Spring 1979.

Hirschowitz, R.G., "The Human Aspects of Managing Transition," *AMACOM,* Vol. 51, No. 3, May - June 1974.

Humble, J.W., "Emerging Nations - A Challenge to Management," *S.A.M. Advanced Management Journal,* New York 34(4), October 1969, pp. 28-38.

Jones, J.E., "The Organizational Universe," *The 1981 Annual Handbook for Group Facilitators,* pp. 155-164.

Koont, Z., "Making Sense of Management Theory," *Harvard Business Review,* Vol. 40, July-August 1962.

Laurent, A., "Dimensions Culturelles des Conceptions de Management," Working paper, INSEAD Fontainebleau, 1980.

Lim, H., "Japanese Management: A Skill Profile," *Training and Development Journal,* October 1981, pp. 18-21.

Livingston, J.S., "Myth of the Well-Educated Manager," *Harvard Business Review,* May-June 1971.

McNulty, N.G., "European Management Education Comes of Age," *The Conference Board Record,* December 1975.

Moris, J.R., "The Transferability of Western Management Concepts and Progress: An East African Perspective," Rockefeller Foundation, New York, March 1977.

Nsekela, A.J., "Educating the International Manager: Some Issues in the African Context," *World Development,* Vol. 8, 1980, pp. 193-204.

Ogranovitch, S., "How to Design an International Training Program," *Training and Development,* August 1980, pp. 12-15.

Pascale, R.T., "Zen and the Art of Management," *Harvard Business Review,* March - April 1978.

Rocchio, R., "Cultural Awareness for Managers," *The Bridge,* Summer 1980, pp. 22-23.

Roche, S., "Coverdale Training: A Method for Developing Managers and the Organization," *Manpower and Applied Psychology,* Vol. 1, No. 1.

Rondinelli, D.A., "Planning Development Projects: Lessons from Developing Countries," *Long-Range Planning,* Vol. 12, June 1973.

Schnapper, M., "A Ten-Step Multinational Training Model," *The Bridge,* Winter 1973, pp. 22-24.

Sherif, A.F., "Developing Public Enterprise Managers: Some Lessons of Experience From the Arab Republic of Egypt," *Coliers Africains D'Administration Publique,* (Tanger) (8), August 1972, pp. 5-38.

Wamalwa, W.N., "Training: The Kenyan Experience," *Coliers Africains D'Administration Publique,* (Tanger) (8), August 1972, 59-66.

Wederspahn, G., "Cultural Awareness," *The Bridge,* Summer 1981.

Wickert, F.R., "Experience-Based Exercises Used for Management Development in Francophone Africa," *Group and Organization Studies,* March 1979, pp. 5-12.

Wigglesworth, D.C., "Management Development Overseas—Some Thoughts," *Training and Development Journal,* October 1981, pp. 73-76.

Youker, R., "Organization Alternatives for Project Managers," *Management Review,* November 1977, pp. 46-53.

(b) **Readings**

Andrew, Kenneth R., *Concept of Corporate Strategy.* Dow-Jones-Irwin, 1971.

Athos, A.G., and Pascale, R.T., *The Art of Japanese Management.* New York: Warner Books, 1981.

Bower, Marvin, *The Will To Manage.* New York: McGraw-Hill Book Company, 1966.

Brannen, T.R. and Hodgson, F.X., *Overseas Management*. New York: McGraw-Hill, 1965.

Brislin, R.W., *Cross-Cultural Encounters*. New York: Pergamon Press, Inc., 1981.

Drucker, Peter F., *The Effective Executive*. New York: Harper & Row Publishers, 1964.

Drucker, Peter F., *Managing for Results: Economic Tasks and Risk-Taking Decisions*. New York: Harper & Row Publishers, 1964.

International Labor Organization, *Zambia: Training of Various Levels of Managerial Personnel*. Geneva, 1973, 23 p.

Jay, A., *Management and Machiavelli*. New York: Holt, Rinehart & Winston, 1967.

Kepner, C.H., & Tregoe, B.B., *The Rational Manager*. New York: McGraw-Hill, 1965.

Leavitt, H.J., *Managerial Psychology*. Chicago: University of Chicago Press, 1965.

Likert, R., *The Human Organization*. New York: McGraw-Hill, 1967.

McNulty, N.G., *Training Managers: The International Guide*. New York: Harper & Row, 1969.

Morrisey, George I., *Management by Objectives and Results*. California: Addison-Wesley Publishing Company, 1970.

Nadler, L., *Developing Human Resources*. Houston: Gulf Publishing Company, 1970.

Odiorne, G.S., *Management by Objectives*. New York: Pitman Publishing Corp., 1965.

Ouchi, W.G., *Theory Z: How American Business can meet the Japanese Challenge*. Reading, Mass: Addison-Wesley, 1981.

Perlmutter, H.V., and Heenan, D.A., *Multinational Organization Development*. Reading, Mass: Addison-Wesley, 1979.

Schein, Edgar H., *Organizational Psychology*. Second Edition. New Jersey: Prentice-Hall, Inc., 1970.

Sedwick, R.C., *Interaction: Interpersonal Relationships in Organizations*. Engelwood Cliffs, NJ: Prentice-Hall, Inc., 1974.

"Leaders, like groups, vary in their characteristics. Different situations and circumstances require different functions to be performed if a group is to move closer to its goal…leadership…is a process."

B.R. Patton, and K. Griffin

Workshop 2
Managerial Styles:
Who is the leader?

---

1. Introduction: In the old days to be a manager was easy and rewarding. Things were relatively simple. You were in charge. You had the authority. You were responsible. You could give orders (were supposed to, as a matter of fact) and they were obeyed. You were born a leader and could improve your leadership through training if you wanted to.

The picture has drastically changed since that "golden" time.

Now, leaders have to cope with ambiguity all the time. What's relevant today is obsolete and inadequate tomorrow. What's effective in one situation is inapplicable in another. Guidelines are not universal any longer. Things are further complicated with the introduction of the intercultural dimension in management. Nowadays, managers have to be aware of cultural differences. They must learn how to cope with people having values, patterns of thinking and behaving which are not easy to understand, to say the least. What a confusion for old-timers and new managers alike.

"Promote and use participation," experts say. And managers do. And it is a failure. People do not want to participate. At least not in all cultures. Let us face it: Who wants to be a leader?

2. Aim: To understand how the managers' styles influence the work and performance of people who belong to various cultures and micro-cultures.

3. Objectives: Participants will:

(a) analyze their managerial styles using a psycho-cultural model (self-assessment exercise, group discussions, and conceptual framework: Input 1);

(b) learn to expand their options and choices regarding leadership and the management of people (role-playing);

(c) examine a set of leadership theories from a cross-cultural perspective (group discussions and conceptual framework: Input 2);

(d) assess their strengths when working in intercultural teams (self-assessment exercise).

4. Process:

Exercise A. Participants go through the self-assessment exercise in the managerial styles provided hereunder:

Managerial Styles: A Self-Assessment Exercise[1]

For each question, circle as spontaneously as possible the right answer (score) for yourself. Do not be afraid of being subjective since the exercise is based on the assumption that you know yourself better than others do. After all, if you don't like the outcome, you still can question it.

	Marginally	Somewhat	Very much
1. Do you enjoy working on new problems?	1	3	5
2. Are you good at noticing what needs attention now in a given situation?	1	3	5
3. Are you a rather unemotional person?	1	3	5
4. Are you interested in other people?	1	3	5
5. Can you predict how other people will react to a proposal?	1	3	5
6. Are you good at analyzing the pros and cons of a proposal?	1	3	5
7. Do you dislike doing the same thing over and over again?	1	3	5
8. Do you rely on past experiences to solve new problems?	1	3	5
9. Are you good at pinpointing flaws in a proposal?	1	3	5
10. Do you let your likes and dislikes interfere in your decisions?	1	3	5

---

[1]This self-assessment exercise is based on *The Collected Works of C.G. Jung,* trans. R.F.C. Hull, Bollingen Series XX. Vol. 6: *Psychological Types,* copyright © 1971 by Princeton University Press, p. 35, as well as on the Briggs Meyer test. See below in conceptual framework: Input 1.

11. Do you perceive the unknown as challenging?	1	3	5
12. Do you usually resent being interrupted when working on a project?	1	3	5
13. Do you perceive yourself as a logical person?	1	3	5
14. Do you enjoy teamwork?	1	3	5
15. Do you have many ups and downs when working?	1	3	5
16. Are you able to keep track of essential details?	1	3	5
17. Do you perceive yourself as a realistic person?	1	3	5
18. Do you put two-and-two together very quickly?	1	3	5
19. Are you good at organizing things?	1	3	5
20. Do you enjoy Public Relations work?	1	3	5

Add up your scores using the following combinations:

Style 1: (a) Questions 2 - 8 - 12 - 16 - 17
(b) Total of scores for the above questions: _____

Style 2: (a) Questions 1 - 7 - 11 - 15 - 18
(b) Total of scores for the above questions: _____

Style 3: (a) Questions 3 - 6 - 9 - 13 - 19
(b) Total of scores for the above questions: _____

Style 4: (a) Questions 4 - 5 - 10 - 14 - 20
(b) Total of scores for the above questions: _____

When the participants have finished adding their scores, the trainer describes the nature of the four managerial styles:[2]

Style 1: Factual. Managers who use this style are basically cool, patient, collected, down-to-earth, oriented to the present, precise, realistic, able to document their statements, sticking to the facts that speak for themselves, *content*-oriented.

Style 2: Intuitive. Intuitive managers are charismatic, imaginative, innovative, creative, future-oriented, quick in their reactions, witty, jumping from one idea to another, *idea*-oriented.

Style 3: Analytical. The analytical style is characterized by a systematic, logical, step-by-step way to look at things, people and ideas. Managers who are strong in this style are looking for options or alternatives to problems, weighing pros and cons, rather unemotional in their approach to management, past, present and future, and *process*-oriented.

Style 4: Normative. Normative managers are *people*-oriented and stress the importance of comunication, relations, teamwork, feelings, emotions, expectations, individuals' uniqueness, understanding, and improvising.

Participants who share the same dominant managerial style (higher scores)[3] meet and clarify its influence on (a) planning; (b) performance appraisal; (c) decision-making; and (d) coaching. (Figure 10. Managerial styles and their cultural features.)

Exercise B. Participants study the interaction between a manager who is "intuitive" (dominant feature) - "analytical" (auxiliary feature) *and* a "factual" (dominant) - "analytical" (auxiliary) team.

First they guess and then, compare their ideas with the following matrix (Figure 11).

Exercise C. The group uses the model on the four managerial styles to approach and understand various cultures from an intercultural viewpoint (Figure 12). They look at the following illustrations, criticize them and then come up with a few of their own. (What about culture specifics?)

---

[2]See P. Casse, *Training for the Cross-Cultural Mind* (Washington, DC: SIETAR, 1980), pp. 160-170; and I. Briggs Meyer, *Introduction to Type* (Palo Alto, CA: Consulting Psychologists Press, Inc., 1976).

[3]Participants who have even scores have to decide which one is more indicative of their dominant managerial style.

Figure 10. Managerial Styles and their Cultural Features

	Factual Style	Intuitive Style	Analytical Style	Normative Style
1. Planning	Focus on the *present*, on the here-and-now. The manager clarifies the existing situation, What is.	Focus on the *future*. The manager sets up objectives.	Relate *past, present* and *future*. The manager works on strategies and tactics.	Focus on the *past*. The manager reviews and assesses what has been done to direct new action.
2. Performance Appraisal	Deal with *skills*. (Register the facts.)	Concentrate on *potential*. (Look for possibilities.)	Assess performance according to *several factors*. (The individual, the situation, the manager, the environment...)	Insist on the performance appraisal *process*, the relationship, the sharing of perceptions. (To understand each other is the aim.)
3. Decision-Making	Decisions are based on facts, and on thorough investigations; they are always well documented.	Decisions are related to hunches, imagination, guesses, trial and error, risk-taking.	Decisions are the end-result of a systematic way to identify options, alternatives and weigh them according to a set of well-analyzed pros and cons.	Decisions are closely linked to the value systems which exist in the team, organization or culture concerned.
4. Coaching	Each individual has to find his or her own way. The manager can only facilitate the process by clarifying the facts.	The manager motivates the employee in describing a "could be" situation appealing to him or her.	Coaching is systematically organized in a kind of step-by-step approach: "This is what has to be done to change what is into what should be."	The basic assumption which underlies the evaluative approach toward coaching is that weaknesses and strengths should be fairly evaluated and taken care of.

Figure 11. The interaction between an Intuitive Manager and a Factual Team

Dominant: Intuitive Manager Auxiliary: Analytical	Dominant: Factual Team Auxiliary: Analytical	Interaction	
		Conflicting	Complementary
• Imaginative and witty	• Wants the facts and thinks things through.	• The manager perceives the team as slow and busy. The team thinks that the leader is too impatient.	• The facts hatch the conceptual construction of reality.
• Sets ambitious objectives. Neglect, "What is" for "What could be".	• Focuses on the current situation. Realism is in order.	• The manager feels that the team resists change. The team believes that the leader is too pushy.	• The objectives are in line with the potential inherent in the situation.
• Analytical and systematic in his or her choices of strategies and tactics.	• Likes to be logical in organizing its activities.	• They can disagree on the right choices of the strategies and tactics. (They are both weak on feeling.)	• The manager and the team are in harmony (too much maybe).
• Enjoys the unforeseen and always ready to cope with new challenges.	• Dislikes improvisation and unplanned action.	• The manager finds the team too rigid. The team perceives the manager as unpredictable.	• The manager learns how to improve the control of his or her activities. The team becomes a little more flexible, adaptable.

Figure 12. Application of the Model on Five Cultures

	EUROPEAN CULTURES	NORTH AMERICAN CULTURES	AFRICAN CULTURES	ASIAN CULTURES	LATIN AMERICAN CULTURES
FACTUAL	• Meanings are in individuals. • Theoretical as opposed to practical • Inconsistent	• Individuals rely on the spoken words. • Professional experiences are perceived as important. • Pragmatic	• Meanings come from the environment. • Time is viewed as flexible. It is not rigid. • "Things" are alive.	• Meanings are everywhere: in people, things.... • There is no clear-cut separation between the internal and external worlds. • Sensing is an illusion.	• Touching is an important part of the communication process. • Sensual • Attracted to poetry, art, literature.
INTUITIVE	• Like to play with ideas. • Creative and imaginative • Enjoy exploring new avenues.	• Look for ideas which can be used. • Enjoy learning. • Can be perceived as "naive" at times (simplistic ideas).	• Superstitious • Ideas come from group interactions. • What is perceived is at least as important as what is.	• Highly "spiritual" • A great sense of unity is shared by many people. • Metaphysical	• Enjoy disagreements on principles, ideas. The stimulation of an exchange of opinions • Jump from one idea to another. • Emotional when talking about possibilities and opportunities.
ANALYTICAL	• Deductive • Rigid organizational structures • Centralized decision-making process	• Inductive • Flexible organization cultures • Decentralized decision-making process	• Are process oriented. • Thinking is highly internalized. (Visual thinking) • Thinking is assimilated to "feeling".	• Accept ambiguity. • Open to many options (there is not just "one way"). • Integrate polarities and contradictions.	• A certain fatalism (Faith is valued) Mañana concept. • Disorganized and highly centralized.
NORMATIVE	• Over-critical • Quality of life is highly valued. • Conflicts are enjoyable.	• Getting the job done is the priority. • People like to be liked at the same time that they "push people around" • Self-esteem is largely based on professional accomplishments	• The concept of kinship is highly valued. • Friendship comes before business and is lasting. • Interpersonal relationships are based on sincerity.	• Simplicity and humility are highly valued. • Peacefulness is what counts above all. • Enjoy flowing with situational forces.	• Machismo (conservative) • Dignita • Personalismo

Exercise D. A role-playing exercise is organized around three phases:[4]

Phase 1.
(1) Four participants are selected to play the role of the managers. They prepare themselves for the interaction with a group of employees (one by one).

(2) At the same time four other members of the group work on their own instructions.

(3) The rest of the group prepares itself for observation.

Instructions for the Four Managers

"Each participant will come to you with an *action plan* to improve the work of the team you are responsible for.

Your behavior will change for each encounter:

Session 1. Be *factual* in your reactions to the employee.

Session 2. Be *intuitive* in responding to the employee's proposals.

Session 3. Be *analytical* in dealing with the action plan proposed by the employee.

Session 4. Be *normative* (people and value oriented) in reacting to the employee's suggestions."

Instructions for the Four Employees

"Assume that you have been asked by your manager to prepare a brief action plan on how to improve the work and effectiveness of the team he or she is responsible for. After you have prepared your plan you will meet with four different managers who will listen and react to your proposal.

---

[4]The use of the video tape recorder can be very effective with exercise.

"Sketch out your action plan in the space below in preparation for your four sessions."

ACTION PLAN FOR IMPROVING TEAM WORK.

Phase 2. When managers and employees are ready (after 15 minutes for preparation) the role-playing starts. One or two observers per employee will move around with the people they are supposed to observe. (The role playing lasts 5 minutes per interaction - Total: 20 minutes.)

Instructions for Observers

Observe the manager's as well as the employees' reactions during the four interactions. You will move along with one of the employees so that you can watch the typical reactions of the four managerial styles.

NOTE FOR INTERACTION 1.

NOTE FOR INTERACTION 2.

NOTE FOR INTERACTION 3.

NOTE FOR INTERACTION 4.

Phase 3. Debriefing of the exercise with the "performers" and the observers:
• Were the managers able to stick to the imposed styles?
• What were the main characteristics of the performed styles?
• What was the impact of each style on the "employees"?
• What can be learned from the role-playing?

Exercise E. Three leadership theories (Models) are examined by the group using a cross-cultural approach:

Figure 13. The Tannenbaum and Schmidt Model[5]

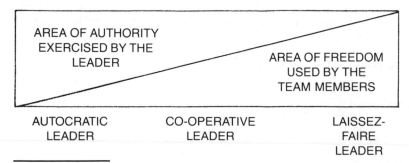

[5]See conceptual framework: Input 2-A.

Issues and Questions for the group:

- Find at least one cultural illustration for each leadership style. (Where do you place the Japanese, French, German, Latin American, and Arabic managers on the scale?)
- Come up with three different cultural ways of "selling" a decision.
- Analyze the interaction between a team that is interested in getting orders and instructions and a manager who wants to involve people in the decision-making process.

Managerial Grid

Figure 14. The Blake and Mouton Grid[6]

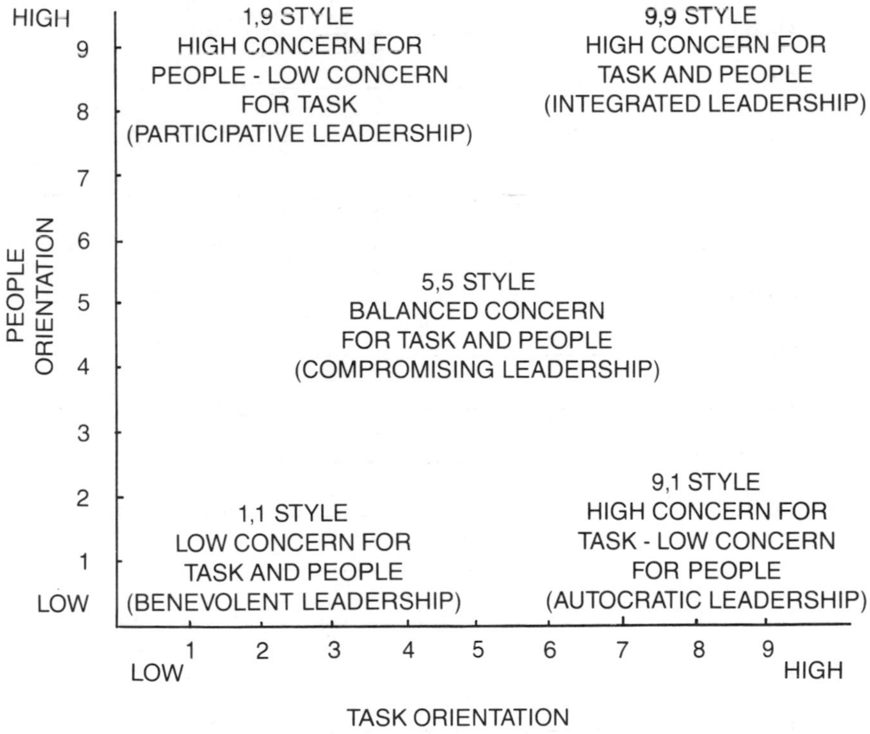

[6]See conceptual framework: Input 2-B as well as R. Blake et. al., "Breakthrough in Organization Development," *Harvard Business Review* (November-December 1964).

Hershey – Situational leadership

3. The Fiedler Approach[7]

Participants take the "test" developed by F.E. Fiedler, M.M. Chemers and L. Mahar.

Instructions

Think of the individual with whom you *work least well* and identify his or her main personality traits on the following 18 scales.

Scoring

	8	7	6	5	4	3	2	1		
Pleasant	8	7	6	5	4	3	2	1	Unpleasant	___
Friendly	8	7	6	5	4	3	2	1	Unfriendly	___
Rejecting	1	2	3	4	5	6	7	8	Accepting	___
Tense	1	2	3	4	5	6	7	8	Relaxed	___
Distant	1	2	3	4	5	6	7	8	Close	___
Cold	1	2	3	4	5	6	7	8	Warm	___
Supportive	8	7	6	5	4	3	2	1	Hostile	___
Boring	1	2	3	4	5	6	7	8	Interesting	___
Quarrelsome	1	2	3	4	5	6	7	8	Harmonious	___
Gloomy	1	2	3	4	5	6	7	8	Cheerful	___
Open	8	7	6	5	4	3	2	1	Guarded	___
Backbiting	1	2	3	4	5	6	7	8	Loyal	___
Untrustworthy	1	2	3	4	5	6	7	8	Trustworthy	___
Considerate	8	7	6	5	4	3	2	1	Inconsiderate	___
Nasty	1	2	3	4	5	6	7	8	Nice	___
Agreeable	8	7	6	5	4	3	2	1	Disagreeable	___
Insincere	1	2	3	4	5	6	7	8	Sincere	___
Kind	8	7	6	5	4	3	2	1	Unkind	___

Total _____

---

[7]F.E. Fiedler, M.M. Chemers and L. Mahar, *Improving Leadership Effectiveness* (New York: John Wiley and Sons, Inc., 1976), p. 8. See conceptual framework: Input 2-C.

Two leadership styles can be assessed through the "test", namely:
1. A leader who is *relationship-motivated* (for a score of 64 or above);
2. A leader who is *task-motivated* (for a score of 57 or below).[8]

The effectiveness of each style is measured according to the *situation* the leader is involved in. Three key situations can be related to the leader's efficiency:

(1) Task-motivated leaders are good at dealing with *low control situations* characterized by the fact the team members do not support their leader, the work to be performed is not clearly defined and the power of the leader is ambiguous.

(2) Task-motivated leaders are also effective when handling *high-control situations* that is to say when he or she has a great deal of control over people (power), a good relationship with the team members and a well-defined task to be performed.

(3) Relationship-motivated leaders are at their best in *moderate control situations* i.e. either a situation with good relations but unclear tasks and low power or with poor relations but clear task and high power.

Issues and questions for the group.

• What does it mean to be a task-motivated leader in a Latin American culture?

• What is the "cultural" meaning of a good relation?

• How can you assess the quality of a situation (low-control, moderate control or high control) in:
— the French culture?
— the North American culture?
— the Japanese culture?
— the Mexican culture?
— the Algerian culture?

Exercise F. The team skill self-assessment exercise.

All the members of the group go through the following self-assessment exercise which has been designed to help them assess their strengths when working in a team.

---

[8]If the score falls between 58-63 the individual has to determine for himself or herself where he or she stands.

Team skills: A self-assessment exercise[9]

Circle the appropriate score for each item:

	Marginally	Somewhat	Very much
Scores:			
1. I like to use my imagination at work.	1	3	5
2. I listen to others.	1	3	5
3. I have a good network of relations.	1	3	5
4. I like to be in charge.	1	3	5
5. I am good at assessing others' ideas.	1	3	5
6. I am successful when organizing things and people.	1	3	5
7. I can translate ideas into actions.	1	3	5
8. I keep track of others' contradictions.	1	3	5
9. I enjoy chairing meetings.	1	3	5
10. I always know where to go to get information.	1	3	5
11. I easily jump from one idea to another.	1	3	5
12. I build upon others' ideas.	1	3	5
13. I am a pragmatic person.	1	3	5
14. I know how to get things done.	1	3	5
15. I am creative.	1	3	5
16. I clarify what has to be done.	1	3	5
17. I like to investigate.	1	3	5
18. I encourage others' participation in a discussion.	1	3	5
19. I am perceived by others as a down-to-earth person.	1	3	5
20. I enjoy discussing strategies and tactics.	1	3	5
21. I evaluate proposals made by team members.	1	3	5
22. My judgement is usually sound.	1	3	5
23. I enjoy searching for facts.	1	3	5
24. I promote good relations in a team.	1	3	5

---

[9]Designed and tested by P. Casse.

	1	3	5
25. I like to establish clear-cut procedures.	1	3	5
26. I can work on many projects at the same time.	1	3	5
27. I am original in my approaches toward problem-solving.	1	3	5
28. I am good at setting up objectives.	1	3	5
29. I am rather factual.	1	3	5
30. I weigh pros and cons of various options before making a decision.	1	3	5
31. I focus more on content (what has to be done) than on process (how to do it).	1	3	5
32. I am rather unemotional.	1	3	5
33. I sometimes overwhelm people with ideas.	1	3	5
34. I know how to ease tensions in a team.	1	3	5
35. I am good at finishing up assignments.	1	3	5
36. I can predict the consequences of various courses of action.	1	3	5
37. I believe in action plans.	1	3	5
38. I like to work on new problems.	1	3	5
39. I strongly believe in teamwork.	1	3	5
40. I usually meet my targets.	1	3	5
41. I see quickly the advantages and disadvantages of a proposal.	1	3	5
42. I am good at exploring ideas.	1	3	5
43. I am problem-solving oriented.	1	3	5
44. I like to direct others.	1	3	5
45. I am innovative.	1	3	5
46. I can be critical of unfounded propositions.	1	3	5
47. I stimulate others' reflection.	1	3	5
48. I am perceived as a very logical individual.	1	3	5
49. I look for implications included in others' ideas.	1	3	5
50. I use the step-by-step approach when working on problems.	1	3	5

51. My assessments are usually thorough.	1	3	5
52. I am very conscientious in my work.	1	3	5
53. I can work with people having different personalities.	1	3	5
54. I clarify roles and responsibilities when working in a team.	1	3	5
55. I process facts in an analytical way.	1	3	5
56. I always try to update my information.	1	3	5
57. I enjoy seeing the outcome of my actions.	1	3	5
58. I like to know the people I work with.	1	3	5
59. I take past, present, and future into account when solving problems.	1	3	5
60. I put two and two together very quickly.	1	3	5
61. I follow up on decisions made by the team.	1	3	5
62. I select priorities well.	1	3	5
63. I usually have practical ideas.	1	3	5
64. I approach problems in a systematic way.	1	3	5
65. I get things done.	1	3	5
66. I am always ready to help others.	1	3	5
67. I can be an effective intermediary between the team and the external environment.	1	3	5
68. I enjoy making decisions.	1	3	5
69. I believe that effective communication is critical in any kind of teamwork.	1	3	5
70. I enjoy experimenting.	1	3	5

Team Skills - Scoring Sheet*

Skill 1. Items	1	11	15	27	33	38	45	47	60	70	
(Scores)	( ) +	( ) +	( ) +	( ) +	( ) +	( ) +	( ) +	( ) +	( ) +	( )	= _____
Skill 2. Items	4	9	16	28	31	43	44	54	62	68	
(Scores)	( ) +	( ) +	( ) +	( ) +	( ) +	( ) +	( ) +	( ) +	( ) +	( )	= _____
Skill 3. Items	5	8	21	22	30	36	41	46	51	64	
(Scores)	( ) +	( ) +	( ) +	( ) +	( ) +	( ) +	( ) +	( ) +	( ) +	( )	= _____
Skill 4. Items	7	13	19	26	35	40	52	57	63	65	
(Scores)	( ) +	( ) +	( ) +	( ) +	( ) +	( ) +	( ) +	( ) +	( ) +	( )	= _____
Skill 5. Items	2	12	18	24	34	39	53	58	66	69	
(Scores)	( ) +	( ) +	( ) +	( ) +	( ) +	( ) +	( ) +	( ) +	( ) +	( )	= _____
Skill 6. Items	6	14	20	25	32	37	48	50	55	59	
(Scores)	( ) +	( ) +	( ) +	( ) +	( ) +	( ) +	( ) +	( ) +	( ) +	( )	= _____
Skill 7. Items	3	10	17	23	29	42	49	56	61	67	
(Scores)	( ) +	( ) +	( ) +	( ) +	( ) +	( ) +	( ) +	( ) +	( ) +	( )	= _____

*For each item report the score which has been selected (1 for marginally, 3 for average, and 5 for very much so). The total cannot be below 10 or above 50.

Figure 15. A Description of Seven Skills and Their Use in Teams

Skill Descriptions	Underused (10 - 20)	Well used (20 - 40)	Overused (40 - 50)
Skill 1. Good at being creative and imaginative	Unimaginative - slow thinker - conservative - use the same approach over and over - low risk taker - prevent the team from experimenting.	Push forward ideas - offer new insights - propose alternatives - discover - stimulate team - innovative - quick thinker.	Go off track - unrealistic - resent criticism - monopolize the discussion - disorganized - overwhelming.
Skill 2. Good at leading and chairing	Passive - a follower - confused about the target - objectives - afraid of giving directions - seek for advice - does not feel responsible - rely on others.	Set up objectives - select priorities - direct - instruct - task and problem-solving oriented - make decisions - clarify responsibilities and roles - chair - is in charge.	Impose his or her ideas on the team - directive - autocratic - sometimes poor use of team resources - too strong - can take advantage of his/her formal role.
Skill 3. Good at monitoring and evaluating	Accept everything without questioning assumptions - cannot pass a judgement on anything - unstable - switch from one position to another without rational reason.	Clarify others' ideas before making any judgement - assess the inputs from others with tact and sensitivity - monitor progress accomplished - keep track of others' contributions - appraise and assess.	Overcritical - tactless - competitive - aggressive - stubborn - lack of receptivity to new ideas.
Skill 4. Good at getting things done	Passive - more interested in ideas than in action - talk too much - forget the task at hand - get off track - postpone implementation - procrastinate.	Transform talk and ideas into practical steps - pragmatic - down-to-earth - consider what is feasible - action-oriented - realistic - achiever.	Act without thinking - do not listen - impatient with theories - lack of flexibility - simplify things - push others - jump from one project to another.
Skill 5. Good at establishing and maintaining good relations	Insensitive to others' feelings - task-oriented - consider people as "resources" - conflictual - bossy - loner.	Listen - support - encourage others - involve everybody in discussions - compromise - teamworker - clarify.	Forget the task at hand - establish good relations for their own sake - waste time in lengthy discussions - disorganized.
Skill 6. Good at processing and organizing teamwork	Do not plan - disorganized - illogical - unsystematic - create confusion - ambiguous - get lost in details - waste time and energy - create moral problems.	Focus on how to - like to organize things - enjoy making policy decisions - see the big picture - put things into perspective - coordinate - keep team on track.	Compete with the leader - over-organize - antagonize the team by his/her forcefulness - too sure of himself/herself - forget details - organize for the sake of organizing.
Skill 7. Good at fact-finding	Feel bad when outside the team - isolated - avoid contacts with non-team members - decide without the facts - cannot document his/her decisions - vague in his/her statements.	Look for facts to prepare sound decisions - able to get support from outside the team - investigate - search - negotiate - is in the middle of a network of contacts.	Go out scouting and forget the team - get trapped into tables and graphs - do not pay enough attention to team members - unemotional.

Participants analyze their scores using the description of the seven skills and their relations to the scores presented in Figure 15.

Issues and questions for the group:

• Identify the composition of an effective inter-disciplinary team.

• What can a multicultural manager do when he or she has too many people with the same skills in the team?

• How can a multicultural manager assess what the team members are good at?

• What is the meaning of the scores close to zero?

Exercise G. Participants meet for 30 minutes in three small teams. Each team must construct a scenario reflecting the main behavioral characteristics of a leader who is to *conduct a meeting* taking the following categories of assumptions into account:

Team A: Assumptions related to the Human Relations Approach

The leader strongly believes in:

(1) **Interdependence and cooperation:** All team members should help each other. Solidarity is a key concept. The main role of the leader is to pool all the team members' resources together.

(2) **Openness:** It is essential for the success of the team that its members be able to express their opinions, positions and feelings as openly as possible. The more open, the more meaningful the teamwork becomes.

(3) **Being "process-oriented":** It is the responsibility of the leader to observe, analyze and facilitate the interactions between the team members. He must be able to sit back and put things into perspective and refer information to the team about its own functioning.

Team B: Assumptions related to the Gestalt Approach

(1) **Individual autonomy:** Each individual is responsible for himself/herself. The better the performance of each team member, the more effective the team is. Each individual must decide alone and be up-front in terms of what he/she thinks and wants to do.

(2) **Conflicts:** Team members should feel free to be agressive. Conflicts are good. They lead to meaningful and creative interaction among team members. Conflicts are necessary to explore the relevance of beliefs, values and assumptions.

(3) **Being "content" oriented:** The leader is directly involved in the substance of any discussion. He/she takes sides, tells where he/she stands and actively participates in the decision-making process. He/she drives himself/herself to share emotions and feelings with team members.

Team C: Assumptions Related to the Provocative Approach

The leader strongly believes in:

(1) **The manager's right to lead:** The focus is placed on the leader himself/herself. One is in charge. One has the right to be oneself and use all communications skills and techniques available (including the provocative one) to achieve one's goals.

(2) **Manipulation:** Communicating is manipulating. The leader will eventually distort, delete, add new meanings, exaggerate, misunderstand on purpose, avoid the issue at stake during the communication process in order to stimulate the team's reflection.

(3) **Being unconventional:** He/she deals with the content as well as the process of teamwork in an innovative, non-conventional way. One forces the team to explore new avenues, to approach a problem in a brand new (unexpected) way. One is negative, humoristic and even sarcastic at the risk of frustrating the team members and having them become aggressive or just withdraw.

When the three teams are ready, they report on their findings and compare the leaders' behavior according to their assumptions.

Issues and Questions:

• Identify at least five of your basic assumptions about leadership and contrast them with their opposites.

• Examine the impact of the three above sets of assumptions in an organization.

• Compare the profiles of the following leaders:
— a Japanese leader,
— a German leader,
— an American leader.

Exercise H. A good self-assessment exercise to be used is the "Leader Effectiveness and Adaptability Description (LEAD)" developed by P. Hersey and K.H. Blanchard and published in the *1976 Annual Handbook for Group Facilitators* (University Associates, pp. 89-99). It provides a four-dimensional model which determines the leadership profile of any individual. It is constructed around the two main dimensions of leading, i.e. the team and relationship orientations. It also takes into consideration the team member's maturity (see Input 3). The assumption of the authors is that the leader's style should be ideally adjusted to the capacity of the team members to master their jobs, take responsibility and learn from their own experience.

5. Time: One or two days.

6. Conceptual Framework:

INPUT 1

Opposite Kinds of Perception and Judgment[10]

The Type Indicator is concerned with the valuable differences in people that result from the way they like to perceive and the way they like to judge. Succeeding at anything takes both perception and judgment. First you have to find out what the problem or situation is and what are the various things you might do about it. Then you have to decide which to do. Finding out is an exercise of perception. Deciding is an exercise of judgment. You have two basic ways of finding out and two basic ways of deciding.

Opposite ways of finding out: sensing and intuition. One way to find out is through your *sensing* (S). *Your eyes and ears and other senses tell you what is actually there and actually happening.* Sensing is especially useful for gathering the facts of a situation. The other way to find out is through your *intuition* (N) which shows you meanings and relationships and possibilities that are beyond the reach of your senses. Intuition is especially useful for seeing what you might do about a situation. You use both sensing and intuition, of course, but not both at once and not, in most cases, with equal liking.

If you like sensing better than intuition, you make more use of sensing, get to be more skillful with it, and grow expert at noticing all the observable facts. You tend to become realistic, practical, observant, fun-loving, and good at remembering a great number of facts and working with them.

If you like intuition better than sensing, you make more use of intuition, get to be more skillful with it, and grow expert at seeing a

---

[10]Reproduced by special permission from *The Introduction to Type* by Isabel Briggs Meyer, copyright 1976. Published by Consulting Psychologists Press Inc., Palo Alto, CA 94306. Further reproduction is prohibited without the publisher's consent.

new possibility or solution. You tend to value imagination and inspirations, and to become good at new ideas, projects and problem-solving.

Opposite ways of deciding: thinking and feeling. One way to decide is through your *thinking* (T). Thinking predicts the logical result of any particular action you may take. Then it decides impersonally, on the basis of cause and effect. The other way to decide is through your *feeling* (F). Feeling takes into account anything that matters or is important to you or to other people (without requiring that it be logical), and decides on the basis of personal values. You use both thinking and feeling, of course, but not both at once and not, in most cases, with equal confidence.

If you trust thinking more than feeling and use it more, you grow to be most skillful in dealing with that part of the world which behaves logically (like machinery) with no unpredictable human reactions. You yourself tend to become logical, objective and consistent, and to make your decisions by analyzing and weighing the facts, including the unpleasant ones.

If you trust and use feeling more than thinking, you grow most skillful in dealing with people. You tend to become sympathetic, appreciative and tactful and to give great weight, when making any decisions, to the personal values that are involved, including those of other people.

The kind of perception you prefer to use, either sensing or intuition, can team up with whichever kind of judgment you prefer to use, either thinking or feeling. So there are four possible combinations, each producing a different set of characteristics—different interests, different values, different needs, different habits of mind and different surface traits.

Your own combination of perception and judgment makes a lot of difference in the kind of work you will do best and enjoy. If your daily work has most need for the kind of perception you naturally prefer, you will handle the job better and find it more satisfying. If your daily work has most need for the kind of deciding that comes naturally to you, your decisions will be better and will be made with more confidence. In choosing among careers, find out how much chance each will give you to use *your own combination of perception and judgment.*

INPUT 2

(A) Dilemmas of Leadership[11]

Our basic dilemma may be a discrepancy between what we believe to be right and desirable and what we do in practice. Maybe we express this as "How democratic can I be?" as opposed to "How authoritarian must I be?" We face a series of dilemmas. For instance,

We have a tradition of competition...but...we must be cooperative.

We are under pressure to get the job done, to be efficient...but...we believe all points of view must be heard.

We are pushed for time...but...we want participative decision-making and this takes time.

We see opportunities for quick results in one-man decisions...but...we believe shared responsibility makes for better solutions.

We can look at the dilemmas in terms of a continuum developed by Warren Schmidt and Robert Tannenbaum.

If we extend the continuum at either extreme we get *autocracy or abdication*. The autocrat violates our traditional values and our self-image as persons who are open and sensitive. The abdicrat is irresponsible and violates concepts of leadership which get work done.

I can decide where I stand on the continuum by examining the following factors:

Forces in me, including:

My motives and needs
My assumptions about people in general and about colleagues, subordinates, superiors, peers, in particular
My value system
My confidence in the group
My leadership inclinations
My feelings of security and my "tolerance for ambiguity"
My own motives as related to the personal needs I am satisfying.

Forces in the group, including:

Their needs for independence/dependence
Their readiness to assume responsibility

---

[11]Reproduced by special permission from *Reading Book for Laboratories in Human Relations Training* by C.R. Mill and L. Porter, "Dilemmas of Leadership," p. 40, copyright 1972, NTL Institute.

Their tolerance for ambiguity
Their interest in the problem
Their understanding of goals and their role in formulating them
Their knowledge, experience, and skill in the particular task
Their expectations
The effect on the group of my own assumptions about them, their
    motives, and needs.

Forces in the situation, including:

Type of organization
Effectiveness of the group
Pressure of time
Consequences of action
The perception I have and the perceptions
    the group has of the task.

An examination of these forces may yield significant information about one's leadership style and, of great importance also, about the way in which that style is appropriate to any given condition created by these forces. There is not one "best" style. Making a decision which affects the well-being of the total group and which the group is going to have to carry out might be done best with a "Consulting" or "Joining" style; but the cry "Man overboard!" requires "Telling". Rather than working hard to develop style *X,* a leader would be wiser to develop the capacity to discern *what kind of leadership is required in a given situation* and the resources to use that style.

Figure 16. Leadership Styles

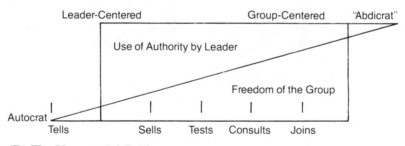

(B) The Managerial Grid

Five leadership styles have been identified and analyzed by Dr. R. Blake and Dr. J. Mouton, namely:

(1) **9,1 Style:** Strong task orientation. The priorities are basically to meet deadlines, get things done, control quality of product or service, tell people what to do and how to do it. Weak emphasis on people and their needs.

(2) **1,1 Style:** Low concern about task and people. Some of the basic assumptions typical of this style are: not wanting to rock the boat, in doubt, wait and see, people can take care of their own business, exposure is dangerous, survival is the name of the game, flow with the forces around.

(3) **1,9 Style:** Strong orientation towards people and their needs and expectations. Managing means "to create the proper environment so that people can perform". Relations, communication and teamwork are the keys for improving productivity.

(4) **5,5 Style:** A moderate concern for team members concerned with a moderate concern for effectiveness. It is the "compromise" approach. The manager in this position believes that the requirements for good productivity can be coupled with the people's needs and expectations.

(5) **9,9 Style:** The team management approach characterized by an integration of a maximum concern for people and a maximum concern for productions. The manager tries to match organizational objectives with individuals' goals. The role of a manager is basically that of a coach.

(C) A Situational Approach to Leadership (Fiedler)

Relationship-motivated leaders have the following reactions (see Figure 17) when they are involved in three different situations:

Figure 17. A Situational Approach to Leadership

SITUATIONS	RELATIONSHIP-MOTIVATED LEADERS	TASK-MOTIVATED LEADERS
1. Low Control Situation: • No support from team members; • Unclear Tasks; • No Power.	They feel stressful - get involved in discussions and consultations - forget the job at hand - are not able to make decisions - are reluctant to alienate their group. POOR PERFORMANCE	Feel comfortable with the challenge of the situation - develop guidelines - get rid of the ambiguity - lead in a forceful way - organize - direct. GOOD PERFORMANCE
2. Moderate Control Situation: • Support from team members but unclear task and lack of power. • Or, poor relations but clear tasks and high power.	They are at their best - Good at dealing with relational issues or tapping the skills and potential of the team members - are sensitive to the team reactions. GOOD PERFORMANCE	They feel out of their element when having to deal with interpersonal conflicts - have a tendency to forget people and their needs - focus too much on the tasks. POOR PERFORMANCE
3. High Control Situation: • Good support from team members; • Clear tasks; • High Power.	They become too concerned with the reactions of their boss and other people outside the team - are less considerate of the team members' feelings - become autocratic, pushy. POOR PERFORMANCE	They are considerate and pleasant-care about people- relax - enjoy - assume an easy-going attitude - they resent interference from others. GOOD PERFORMANCE

INPUT 3

The situational leadership approach developed by Hersey and Blanchard is a dynamic one in the sense that they believe that a leader has to adjust himself or herself to the team members' *maturity* on the job.

On-the-job maturity is defined as the team members' ability to:
(a) set high but realistic objectives;
(b) take responsibility;
(c) acquire experience and learn from it.

The theory claims that as the level of the team members' maturity increases in relation to a task on a job, the leader should reduce his or her task behavior and reinforce his or her process behavior.

7. Handouts and Readings:

(a) Handouts

Baker, B.N., and Wilemon, D.L., "A Summary of Major Research Findings Regarding the Human Element in Project Management," *Project Management Quarterly,* Vol. VIII, No. 1, March 1977.

Blake, R.R., and Mouton, J.S., "What's New with the Grid?," *Training and Development Journal,* May 1978.

Blake, R.R., and Mouton, J.S., "An Overview of the Grid," *Training and Development Journal,* May 1975.

Boone, T.A., "A Practical Leadership Paradigm," *The 1977 Annual Handbook for Group Facilitators.*

Bowen, W., "Almost Everything You Ever Wanted to Know about Leadership," *Fortune,* June 1974.

Briggs Meyer, I., "Introduction to Types," Gainesville, Florida: Center for Applications of Psychological Type, 1976.

England, G.W., "Personal Value Systems of American Managers," *Academy of Management Journal,* 10 (1967), pp. 53-68.

Fiedler, F.E., "The Contingency Model - New Directions for Leadership Utilization," *The Journal of Contemporary Business,* Vol. 3, No. 4, Autumn 1974, pp. 65-80.

Fiedler, F.E., "The Effect of Leadership and Cultural Heterogeneity on Group Performance: A Test of the Contingency Model," *Journal of Experimental Social Psychology,* 2 (1966), pp. 237-64.

Fiedler, F.E., "Style or Circumstances: The Leadership Enigma," *Psychology Today,* March 1969.

Gabarro, J.J., and Kotter, J.P., "Managing your Boss," *Harvard Business Review,* January-February 1980.

Hersey, P., and Blanchard, K.H., "The Management of Change," *Training and Development Journal,* June 1980, pp. 80-98.

Hersey P., and Blanchard, K.H., "Leadership Style: Attitudes and Behaviors," *Training and Development Journal,* May 1982, pp. 50-52.

Holt, D.A., and de Olivares, J.M., "A Model for Management," *Creative Management,* 1979.

Levinson, H., "The Abrasive Personality," *Harvard Business Review,* May-June 1978.

L'Herisson, L., "Making the Most of Your Intuitions," *Training and Development Journal,* April 1981, pp. 111-114.

Pelz, D.C., "Leadership Within a Hierarchical Organization," *Journal of Social Issues,* Vol. VII, 1951.

Peters, T.J., "Leadership: Sad Facts and Silver Linings," *Harvard Business Review,* November-December 1979.

Reddin, W.J., "The 3-D Management Style Theory," *Training and Development Journal,* June 1979, pp. 62-67.

Tannenbaum, R., and Schmidt, W.H., "How to Choose a Leadership Pattern," *Harvard Business Review,* May-June 1973.

Tregoe, B., "Today's Leader- An Endangered Species," *Training and Development Journal,* June 1976.

Vroom, V.H., "Can Leaders Learn to Lead?," Paper delivered at the 1975 annual meeting of the American Psychological Association.

Weiss, A., "Leadership Styles: Which are Best When?," *Supervisory Management,* January 1976.

Wood, J.T., "Leadership as Persuasion and Adaptation," *The 1976 Annual Handbook for Group Facilitators.*

Zaleznik, A., "The Human Dilemmas of Leadership," *Harvard Business Review,* July-August 1963.

(b) Readings

Argyris, C., *Executive Leadership.* New York: Harper and Row, 1953.

Argyris, C., *Increasing Leadership Effectiveness.* New York: John Wiley and Sons, 1976.

Bahm, A.J., *Comparative Philosophy.* World Books, 1977.

Bass, B., *Leadership, Psychology and Organizational Behavior.* New York: Harper, 1960.

Blake, R., and Mouton, J., *Corporate Excellence Through Grid Organization Development.* Houston: Gulf Publishing Company, 1968.

Blake, R., and Mouton, J., *Building a Dynamic Corporation Through Grid Organization Development.* Reading, Mass: Addison-Wesley, 1969.

Blake, R., and Mouton, J., *The Managerial Grid.* Houston: Gulf Publishing Company, 1964.

Condon, J., and Kurata, K., *In Search of What's Japanese About Japan.* Tokyo: Schufunotomo, 1974.

Dimock, H.G., *Leadership and Group Development Series.* San Diego, California: Learning Resources Corporation, 1970.

Fiedler, F.E., *A Theory of Leadership Effectiveness.* New York: McGraw Hill, 1967.

Fiedler, F.E., and Chemers, M.M., *Leadership and Effective Management.* Glenview, Illinois: Scott, Foresman and Company, 1974.

Fiedler, F.E., Chemers, M.M., Mahar, L., *Improving Leadership Effectiveness: The Leader Match Concept.* New York: John Wiley and Sons, Inc., 1976.

Guest, R.H. Hersey P., and Blanchard, H., *Organizational Change Through Effective Leadership.* San Diego, California: Learning Resources Corporation, 1977.

Harris, P.R., and Moran, R.T., *Managing Cultural Differences.* Houston: Gulf Publishing Company, 1979.

Herman, S.M., and Korenich, M., *Authentic Management: A Gestalt Orientation to Organizations and Their Development.* Reading, Mass: Addison-Wesley, 1977.

Hersey, P., and Blanchard, K.H., *Management of Organizational Behavior.* Englewood Cliffs, NJ: Prentice-Hall, 1977.

Hitti, P.K., *Islam - A Way of Life.* Gateway Editions, 1970.

Hunt, J.G., and Larson, L.L. (eds.), *Crosscurrents in Leadership.* Carbondale, Illinois: Southern Illinois University Press, 1979.

Hunt, J.G., and Larson, L.L. (eds.), *Leadership Frontiers.* Carbondale, Illinois: Southern Illinois University Press, 1975.

Lassey, W.R., (ed.), *Leadership and Social Change.* Iowa City: University Associates, 1973.

Likert, R., *New Patterns of Management*. New York: McGraw-Hill, 1961.

McGregor, D., *The Human Side of Enterprise*. New York: McGraw-Hill Book Company, 1960.

McGregor, D., *The Professional Manager*. New York: McGraw-Hill, 1967.

Patai, R., *The Arab Mind*. New York: Scribner, 1973.

Pearson, R.P. (ed.), *Through Middle Eastern Eyes*. Cambridge: Praeger, 1975.

Reischauer, E.O., *The Japanese*. Cambridge: Harvard University Press, 1977.

Rivera, J., *Latin America: A Sociocultural Interpretation*. Irvington: Halsted Press, 1978.

Stogdill, R.M., *Handbook of Leadership: A Survey of Theory and Research*. New York: The Free Press, 1974.

Tannenbaum R., et. al., *Leadership and Organization: A Behavioral Approach*. New York: McGraw-Hill, 1961.

Tannenbaum, R., Weschler, I., and Massarik F., *Leadership and Organization: A Behavorial Science Approach*. New York: McGraw-Hill Book Co., 1961.

Tead, O., *The Art of Leadership*. New York: McGraw-Hill, 1965.

Vroom, V.H., and Yetton, P.W., *Leadership and Decision-Making*. Pittsburgh: University of Pittsburgh Press, 1973.

Whyte, W.H., *The Organization Man*. New York: Simon and Schuster, 1956.

Wiener, P.P., (ed.), *Ways of Thinking of Eastern Peoples: India, China, Tibet, Japan*. Honolulu: University Press of Hawaii, 1964.

"Where the social symbols provide an effective channel for the individual in terms of his particular phychological traits, the psychic energies flow out smoothly toward life."

I. Progroff

Workshop 3
Motivation Across Cultures:
Can we motivate people?

1. Introduction: Motivation is critical for the multi-cultural manager. He or she has to know how to understand people's motives and manage them accordingly in order to be as effective as possible economically, socially, and *culturally* speaking. It seems to me many managers in many cultures are behaving according to three false assumptions, namely:

(1) that people can be motivated if the appropriate actions are taken;

(2) that the motivation theories of the 1950's are still valid today;

(3) that people with different cultural backgrounds share some basic needs in common. All people are thus essentially alike.

About the first assumption, I would suggest that one does not motivate people but one *helps* people *motivate themselves*. The difference is quite important!

Regarding the motivation theories designed 30 years ago, I think it is time to realize that people and social environments have changed. New theories which are more relevant to what people want and need exist. These theories could be used by the managers.

Finally, it is quite true that human beings do share in common some basic needs. But the point is that those needs are valued differently according to various cultures and that the cultural expressions or actualizations of those needs also differ from one culture to another.

2. Aim: To approach *motivation* and *motivation theories* from an intercultural perspective.

3. Objectives: Participants will:

(a) define motivation cross-culturally (group discussion and exercise);

(b) analyze two motivation theories using a cross-cultural approach (group discussions, exercises and conceptual framework: Inputs 1 and 2);

(c) study three basic needs and their cultural expressions (exercise and group discussion);

(d) reflect on the management of motivation (case study and conceptual framework: Input 3);

(e) experience a cross-cultural way to look at motivation (self-assessment exercise and group discussion);

(f) use a "psycho-cultural" approach towards motivation (self-assessment exercise, group discussion and Input 4).

4. Process:

Exercise A. The following definition is given to the group which analyzes its cultural dimension (values, beliefs, and assumptions included in the definition):

"Motivation is characterized by a set of internal and external driving forces which activate, channel, and sustain behavior towards some individual group, and organizational and societal goals."

The discussion centers around the cultural meaning of:

- activate (Does it mean create?)
- channel (Is the implication that the forces color the individual's personality?)
- sustain (Do the driving forces provide consistency and continuity?)
- behavior (What is behavior? Is speaking behaving?)
- individual goals (Are these goals related to the pleasure principle?)
- group goals (Who decides on the group goals?)
- organizational goals (Are they contingent on the organizational culture?)
- societal goals (What is the impact of the social system on the driving forces?)

The next step is for the group to react to the adapted Vroom's equation:

$$M = F \, \frac{P\,(R)}{P\,(E)}$$

An individual's motivation is the function of the relation between his or her perception of both the expected reward and the effort to be made to get that reward.

Exercise B. The group looks at the picture and answers the question: *Why is the man doing what he is doing?* (30 minutes)

Man at Work: His Motivations[1]

[1]J.D. Hess, *From the Other's Point of View* (Scottdale, PA: Herald Press, 1980), p. 65.

The answers are recorded by the trainer on a flipchart and discussed by the participants who try to pinpoint as many cultural assumptions as possible:

Motives can be identified as follows:

(1) to make a living
(2) to serve people
(3) to help the community
(4) to please God
(5) to avoid punishment
(6) to improve his situation
(7) to make money
(8) to disseminate information
(9) to send his children to school
(10) to get recognition from his fellow citizens.
    others...

Exercise C. This part of the workshop is conducted in four phases:

Phase 1. The following motivation feedback questionnaire is administered to the participants.[2]

Directions

The following statements have seven possible responses.

Strongly Agree	**Agree**	**Slightly Agree**	**Don't Know**	**Slightly Disagree**	**Disagree**	**Strongly Disagree**
+3	+2	+1	0	-1	-2	-3

Please mark one of the seven responses by circling the number that corresponds to the response that fits your opinion. For example: if you "Strongly Agree", circle the number " + 3".

Complete every item. You have about 10 minutes to do so.

1. Special wage increases should be given to employees who do their jobs very well. +3 +2 +1 0 -1 -2 -3
2. Better job descriptions would be helpful so that employees will know exactly what is expected of them. +3 +2 +1 0 -1 -2 -3
3. Employees need to be reminded that their jobs are dependent on the Company's ability to compete effectively. +3 +2 +1 0 -1 -2 -3

---

[2]Reprinted from: J.E. Jones and J.W. Pfeiffer (Eds.), *The 1973 Annual Handbook for Group Facilitators*. San Diego, CA: University Associates, 1973. Used with permission.

4. A supervisor should give a good deal   +3 +2 +1 0 -1 -2 -3
of attention to the physical working
conditions of his employees.

5. The supervisor ought to work hard to   +3 +2 +1 0 -1 -2 -3
develop a friendly working atmos-
phere among his people.

6. Individual recognition for above-   +3 +2 +1 0 -1 -2 -3
standard performance means a lot to
employees.

7. Indifferent supervision can often   +3 +2 +1 0 -1 -2 -3
bruise feelings.

8. Employees want to feel that their real   +3 +2 +1 0 -1 -2 -3
skills and capacities are put to use on
their jobs.

9. The Company retirement benefits   +3 +2 +1 0 -1 -2 -3
and stock programs are important
factors in keeping employees on their
jobs.

10. Almost every job can be made more   +3 +2 +1 0 -1 -2 -3
stimulating and challenging.

11. Many employees want to give their   +3 +2 +1 0 -1 -2 -3
best in everything they do.

12. Management could show more inter-   +3 +2 +1 0 -1 -2 -3
est in the employees by sponsoring
social events after hours.

13. Pride in one's work is actually an   +3 +2 +1 0 -1 -2 -3
important reward.

14. Employees want to be able to think of   +3 +2 +1 0 -1 -2 -3
themselves as "the best" at their own
jobs.

15. The quality of the relationships in   +3 +2 +1 0 -1 -2 -3
the informal work group is quite
important.

16. Individual incentive bonuses would   +3 +2 +1 0 -1 -2 -3
improve the performance of
employees.

17. Visibility with upper management   +3 +2 +1 0 -1 -2 -3
is important to employees.

18. Employees generally like to schedule   +3 +2 +1 0 -1 -2 -3
their own work and to make job-
related decisions with a minimum of
supervision.

19. Job security is important to   +3 +2 +1 0 -1 -2 -3
employees.

20. Having good equipment to work with   +3 +2 +1 0 -1 -2 -3
is important to employees.

Phase 2. The Maslow theory on human needs is briefly presented to the participants (see conceptual framework: Input 1 and Figure 18).

Figure 18. The Maslow Theory on Human Needs

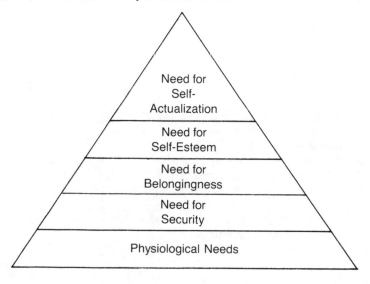

Phase 3. Each participant scores his or her own answers to the 20 questions.

Scoring

1. Transfer the numbers you circled in Phase 1 to the appropriate places in the chart below:

Statement No.	Score	Statement No.	Score
10	————	2	————
11	————	3	————
13	————	9	————
18	————	19	————
Total (Self-Actualization Needs)	————	Total (Safety Needs)	————

Statement No.	Score	Statement No.	Score
6	_____	1	_____
8	_____	4	_____
14	_____	16	_____
17	_____	20	_____
Total (Esteem Needs)	_____	Total (Basic Needs)	_____

Statement No.	Score
5	_____
7	_____
12	_____
15	_____
Total (Belonging Needs)	_____

2. Record your total scores in the chart below by marking an "X" in each row next to the number of your total score for that area of needs motivation.

	−12	−10	−8	−6	−4	−2	0	+2	+4	+6	+8	+10	+12
Self-Actualization													
Esteem													
Belonging													
Safety													
Basic													

Low Use   High Use

Once you have completed this chart, you can see the relative strength of your use of each of these areas of needs motivation.

There is, of course, no "right" answer. What is right for you is what matches the actual needs of your employees and that, of course, is specific to each situation and each individual. In general, however, the "experts" tell us that today's employees are best motivated by efforts in the areas of Belonging and Esteem.

Phase 4. Five issues are critically examined by the participants who work in trios:

1. Is the hierarchy of needs identical for all cultures?

2. Are the needs culturally expressed the same way? Do they mean the same thing to different people?

3. Is it universally true that the basic needs have to be met before the more "sophisticated" needs, such as the need for self-actualization?

4. What about the relationships between the various needs? Aren't they closely interrelated in some cultures? Isolated in others?

5. Can the group identify a culture for each need?

Some typical reactions are:

1. No, the needs can be ranked in a different way according to the value system which exists in a given culture.

2. No, the needs can be perceived and internalized differently by various groups, communities, countries.

3. Quite true. A problem with the need for security can lead to anxiety, but be at the same time an opportunity for self-actualization.

4. North American for physiological (meaning materialistic) needs, Russian for security, Latin American for belongingness, French for self-esteem (ego status), and Eastern cultures for self-actualization.

Exercise D. The essentials of Herzberg's theory on motivation are introduced to the group as follows:

Phase 1. Participants are asked to answer two questions on an individual basis (they write their responses on a small card distributed by the trainer).

Question 1: "Try to remember a situation in your professional past which gave you *great satisfaction*."

Question 2: "Try to remember a situation in your professional past which gave you *great dissatisfaction*."

Phase 2. The Herzberg theory on hygiene factors and motivators is presented by the trainer (see conceptual framework: Input 2 and Figure 19).

Figure 19. The Herzberg Theory on Motivation[3]

JOB DISSATISFACTION	JOB SATISFACTION
ENVIRONMENT	WORK
Organization policies and administration Supervision Working conditions Interpersonal relationships Money, status, security	Achievement Recognition Work itself Responsibility Professional growth
Hygiene factors	Motivators

Phase 3. Participants meet in small groups and:

(1) exchange ideas about the correlations between their answers to the two questions and the theory;

(2) analyze the *validity* of the theory (Herzberg claims that the theory is applicable to all individuals and cultures!) Three cross-cultural issues can be tackled by the group members:

• What about a culture in which the working environment is more important than the work itself? (Find examples.)

• Is it correct that all "motivators" (such as an opportunity to achieve, the right recognition at the right time, etc.) create satisfaction in all cultures? (Document your statements.)

• Is job satisfaction always a source of increased productivity? (Identify pro or con arguments.)

Phase 4. At this point in the workshop, it is good to try to compare the two theories (Maslow's and Herzberg's):

— the three first needs (physiological, security, and belongingness or social) correspond to the hygiene factors (environment).

— the two last needs of the Maslow's hierarchy are related to the "motivators".

Exercise E. Participants are invited to leave the room and to come back one by one and go through the following exercise:

Each individual is told that he/she has to throw as many paper balls as possible into the waste basket selecting only one distance or point from which he or she is going to throw them (Figure 20).

---

[3]A film on Dr. F. Herzberg's theory can be used for this workshop. It is called "Motivation through Job Enrichment" and has been produced by BNA Communications. The film has a case study (a dialogue between a manager and an employee) which can be very helpful when demonstrating the theory.

Figure 20. The Paper Ball Simulation[4]

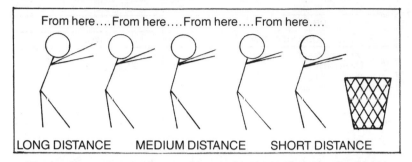

LONG DISTANCE   MEDIUM DISTANCE   SHORT DISTANCE

The trainer must make sure that (1) the exact same instructions are provided to all participants; (2) participants who have been through the exercise remain silent while a new member goes through it; (3) the point which is selected by each participant is recorded in terms of being "L" for long distance, "M" for medium distance and "S" for short distance;[5] (4) the "performers" do not realize that what is important in the exercise is *not* the number of paper balls that he or she can throw into the waste basket but the *distance* between the thrower and the waste basket.

When all participants have finished the simulation, the trainer proposes the following self-assessment exercise on motivation:

Motivation: A Self-Assessment Exercise[6]

For each item, select as spontaneously as possible the right answer (score) for yourself taking into account your work situation. Check the appropriate score.

	Not at all	Moderately so	Very much so
1. I enjoy working in teams.	1	3	5
2. I respect authority.	1	3	5
3. I take calculated risks.	1	3	5
4. I value prestige.	1	3	5
5. I like to work on my own.	1	3	5

---

[4]Adapted from an exercise created by Dr. D. McClelland from Harvard University.

[5]After each shot the trainer asks the person involved to remember his or her assigned letter, namely M, L or S, according to their selection.

[6]Created by P. Casse using D. McClelland's theory.

6. I enjoy creative teamwork.	1	3	5
7. I believe in order and organization.	1	3	5
8. I am always ready to help others.	1	3	5
9. I feel responsible for my own actions.	1	3	5
10. I feel like an "integrator."	1	3	5
11. I like to be appreciated by others.	1	3	5
12. I enjoy being involved in important projects.	1	3	5
13. I like interacting with others.	1	3	5
14. I always try to enhance my performance.	1	3	5
15. I feel like an entrepreneur.	1	3	5
16. I focus on communication when working with others.	1	3	5
17. I think I am good at managing others' work.	1	3	5
18. I value cooperation.	1	3	5
19. I enjoy challenging assignments.	1	3	5
20. I like to give direction to others.	1	3	5
21. I respect others' needs and expectations.	1	3	5
22. I enjoy being effective.	1	3	5
23. I think I am good at getting people working together on a project.	1	3	5
24. I appreciate the right recognition for a job well done.	1	3	5
25. I value friendship.	1	3	5
26. I like to set up my own working goals.	1	3	5
27. I think that leadership is critical in all work situations.	1	3	5
28. I am creative and innovative.	1	3	5
29. I enjoy giving advice to people.	1	3	5
30. I want to know how well I perform.	1	3	5

SCORING

Place the score next to the corresponding number. Then, add up your total score for each motivation.

Motivation 1: (a) Items:		Motivation 2: (a) Items:		Motivation 3: (a) Items:	
3	____	1	____	2	____
5	____	6	____	4	____
9	____	10	____	7	____
14	____	11	____	8	____
15	____	13	____	12	____
19	____	16	____	17	____
22	____	18	____	20	____
26	____	21	____	24	____
28	____	23	____	27	____
30	____	25	____	29	____

(b) Total
    Score:
	_____	(b) Total
		    Score:
			_____	(b) Total
				    Score:
					_____

When all participants have finished the self-assessment exercise, the trainer then explains the theory (McClelland's) behind the two previous exercises.

• The Paper Ball Simulation

People who select the medium distance (M) have apparently a *need for Achievement* [n(Ach)] because they chose a point which is characterized by the fact that: (a) they have a good chance to succeed in throwing the paper balls in the waste basket and (b) it is still challenging enough to be appealing to them.

People who throw the paper balls from the short distance (S), meaning from almost above the waste basket, are basically trying to please the trainer and have a *need for Affiliation* [n(Aff)].

People who try to do the exercise from the farthest point (longer distance: L) have a *need for Power* [n(Pow)] and are in a way interested in impressing (getting the attention of) the trainer as well as the other participants.

• The Self-Assessment Exercise

Motivation 1 is the need for *achievement* n(Ach).

Motivation 2 is the need for *affiliation* n(Aff).

Motivation 3 is the need for *power* n(Pow).

Figure 21. Motivation Profile   (An illustration)

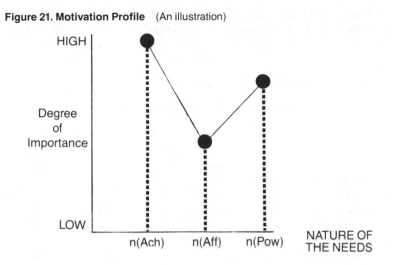

Each individual in the group plots his or her profile. The major psychological characteristics of each need have been described by D. McClelland as:

(1) **Achievement-oriented people** are people who always want to perform better, improve a given situation, set their own goals, like moderate risks but at the same time challenging situations (not too easy or too difficult), take personal responsibility for their own actions, seek feedback regarding their behavior and do things in a creative and innovative way. They are *entrepreneurs*.

(2) **Affiliation-oriented people** like to interact with others, enjoy mutual friendship, get involved in group projects. They like to be liked and appreciated and are more effective when working with others in a cooperative spirit. They are sensitive to other people's needs. They are *team workers*.

(3) **Power-oriented people** like power for its own sake, for the benefit of the team or the organization they belong to or for both at the same time. They like to influence or have an impact on other people. They are attracted by prestigious activities and highly sensitive to status and formal recognition. They enjoy directing others and giving instruction as well as providing help (sometimes without being requested to do so). They are *leaders*.

The next task for the participants is to match their motivation profile with their work or job profile. This can be done in three phases:

Phase 1. The trainer asks the participants to rank their work and its main tasks using the three above descriptions of each need. (See Figure 22.)

Figure 22. Outline of a Work Attribute Role

Please choose the appropriate response.

	Not at all	Moderately so	Very much so
Scores:	(2)	(6)	(10)
Is your work achievement-oriented?			
1. How much freedom do you have in setting up your own objectives?	2	6	10
2. How challenging is your work?	2	6	10
3. Does your work provide clear feedback about the quality of your performance?	2	6	10
4. How much creativity do you have to use on the job?	2	6	10
5. How good are your chances to accomplish your objectives?	2	6	10
TOTAL OF THE SCORES:			
Is your work affiliation-oriented?			
1. Does your job provide an opportunity to work with others in a stable way?	2	6	10
2. To what extent do you need others to succeed in your job?	2	6	10
3. How much time do you have for personal contact with others when working?	2	6	10
4. Is your job integrated into a team effort?	2	6	10
5. How many people can you interact with in the working area?	2	6	10
TOTAL OF THE SCORES:			

Is your work power-oriented?

1. How much opportunity do you have to personally direct others?	2	6	10
2. How prestigious is your work?	2	6	10
3. How much control do you have over your work?	2	6	10
4. How "political" is your work (from an organizational viewpoint)?	2	6	10
5. How much critical information does your work provide to you?	2	6	10

TOTAL OF THE SCORES: ⎯⎯⎯⎯ ⎯⎯⎯⎯ ⎯⎯⎯⎯

GRAND TOTAL: ⎯⎯⎯⎯ ⎯⎯⎯⎯ ⎯⎯⎯⎯

Phase 2. An illustration of the matching process is given to the group by the trainer (See Figure 23).

Figure 23. Matching Needs and Work Attributes (An illustration)

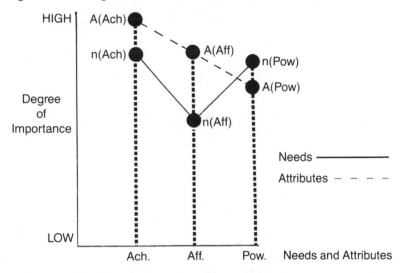

In this case, the need for achievement is inferior to the corresponding attribute; the need for affiliation is also less important than the corresponding work attribute; and the need for power is higher than what the work requires.

A discussion about the possible implications of the match is conducted by the trainer. It focuses upon:

• the fact that according to D. McClelland, it is much easier to raise the importance of a need (through training, for instance) than to decrease it;

• the possibilities to modify the work attributes (job enrichment);

• the *fears* and *frustrations* which can stem from the gaps which exist between what the individual wants and the job requirements;

• the use of other team members to meet the job requirements (delegation of authority, new distribution of responsibility, the matrix approach);

• the alternative to go outside the organization to fulfill the needs which are not met on the job.

Phase 3. The intercultural aspects of the theory are examined by the participants who try to:

(1) set up a stereotype profile for three selected cultures *(North American:* achievement-power-affiliation; *Latin American:* affiliation-power-achievement; *Russian:* power-affiliation-achievement);

(2) determine the nature of the interactions between people who belong to cultures which value different needs, i.e., strong achievement versus strong affiliation...;

(3) analyze how the profiles of different cultures have changed through history (e.g., Roman, Greek, Arabic cultures).

Exercise F. The following case study is (1) read by the participant individually; (2) discussed in small group and (3) discussed in a plenary session (one hour).

CASE STUDY: MANAGING MOTIVATION[7]

Bjørn Sorgenfeldt was disturbed. His mission to Ghana for the Intercultural Development Bank (IDB) to assess the Ministry of Transportation's request for a 50 million dollar loan to construct a road from Accra, the capital, to Kumasi, a major manufacturing city some 250 miles northwest, was experiencing problems. He was unsure what was the cause of the difficulties. He believed that a large part of the problem lay in the relationship between mission team members and decided to call

---

[7]This case has been created by Dr. S. Rhinesmith. All names and incidents are pure fiction.

a meeting of his colleagues to discuss the matter. In preparing for the meeting, he was reviewing the situation as it had developed during the two weeks since the team had arrived in the country.

The other members of the team were typical of an IDB mission like this. They came from a variety of national backgrounds and represented a range of occupational expertise. Four of the other five like Bjørn were from within the Bank. The fifth was an American expert who had been recruited because of his special knowledge and understanding of the Ghanaian manufacturing and marketing system and its potential.

Eduardo Caballero, a Colombian with strong credentials in road construction was the major technical specialist on the mission. He had been working with the Ministry of Transportation and was zeroing in on the plan which the Ministry had developed for the road. It was a difficult task, because between Accra and Kumasi the topography changed as the broad higher land of the coastal area drifted off into heavy rain forest which was impenetrable at some points. The particular route chosen by the Ministry was in question, because there were indications that local tribal desires for accessibility to a main thoroughfare had been more highly considered in selecting the route than had considerations of terrain.

Eduardo was an easy-going person who enjoyed being with people and got along very well with his Ghanaian counterparts, even though they had occasional disagreements regarding technical matters. He enjoyed meeting with other team members in the evenings at the Ambassador Hotel and would encourage the other members, especially Aziz Tanod, an Indonesian economist with the mission, to stay up late, talking about experiences they had had over their years with the Bank.

Aziz Tanod also enjoyed the evenings spent together with Eduardo and other team members. He was sorry and sometimes frustrated, however, by the fact that Bjørn always seemed to want to break up the evening earlier than Aziz and Eduardo.

Bjørn argued that they were under great time pressure and that it was important that everyone not only be in good physical condition for work each day, but spend the time necessary each evening to review the day's findings, prepare analyses and develop new areas of investigation for the next day. Bjørn seemed to Aziz to be overly concerned with the substance of the mission and to have little concern or understanding of the necessity of getting to know other mission members and Ghanaian counterparts on a social level in order to ensure the success of the project.

At the same time, Aziz understood that Bjørn was under considerable pressure from Headquarters in Washington which was particularly interested in the results of this mission. Bjørn's Division had experienced difficulty with the last transportation mission to Ghana and the recommendation of the mission and had been turned down by the Executive Committee. His Division Chief, smarting over the failure last time, had told Bjørn before he left that the report of this mission would need to not only meet, but exceed the standards normally set by the Bank for its project personnel.

In addition to this pressure, Bjørn was trying to deal with Bernard Dupre and Raj Mathuri, two other team members who appeared very driven by the project and with whom there were from time to time sharp confrontations over the exact way in which the mission should proceed. Bernard Dupre was a French Financial Analyst who was the senior member of the mission, having served with the Bank for more than 15 years. During that time he had never been assigned as a mission team leader, having refused numerous offers with the explanation that he felt it was important to "get the job done" and that the "handholding" required for team members was something that he did not want to be bothered with. He contended that he had been hired by the Bank for his financial expertise, not his "nurturing spirit" and he intended to perform the role for which he had been chosen. He didn't have much patience with team leaders who spent a lot of time socializing with team members, but was willing to let them do it, just so they wouldn't "pull him into it," and would stay clear of him so he could do his work.

Raj Mathuri was an economist who did not particularly care for Dupre's "loner" style of operating, but agreed with his concern that Sorgenfeldt, the Mission leader, spent too much time requiring evening meetings to "coordinate the project". He secretly believed that Sorgenfeldt was so nervous about the project, given the pressures of his Division Chief back in Washington, that he overcontrolled the project and the mission members. Mathuri had led many missions himself and had gained a reputation as a forceful leader who, while he tended to be a little overbearing and self-centered, always got the job done. Having been educated in a British school system, Mathuri had an excellent command of written as well as spoken English. While he spoke with a heavy accent which was difficult for others to understand when he got excited, he was by far the most dynamic member of the team.

John Anderson, the American specialist in Ghanaian manufacturing and marketing, had been a Peace Corps Volunteer in Ghana prior to returning to the United States and obtaining his MBA at Stanford. He was the youngest member of the team by far and had been selected by the Bank as an outside expert because he had developed a unique expertise unavailable through traditional educational channels. This was his first Bank mission and he wanted very much to succeed, since it would be a very important addition to his credentials as a consultant. He liked Bjørn and spent a great deal of time with him, asking questions about the Bank and trying to better understand the work the Bank was doing in other areas outside the transportation section. Since Sorgenfeldt had just finished a general economic mission to Ghana only the year before, he had a broad overview of the Ghanaian economic picture. Anderson enjoyed sitting at the Ambassador Bar in the evening after the meeting asking Bjørn questions about the Bank while Eduardo and Aziz talked about the missions they had been on.

When Bjørn called the special meeting for that evening, John was surprised. He had felt the mission was going well. He had been learning a lot and had had a great deal of fun. He had heard, however, that Raj had been increasingly concerned about Eduardo's and Aziz's attitude and late-night discussions and believed that Bjørn was neither handling the team right nor setting the right example for leadership. As a result, Bjørn called the special meeting in order to deal with Raj's questions.

When they entered the comfortable room in the hotel which had served as the main meeting room for the mission group, Mathuri and Dupre were shocked to discover that Eduardo had invited two Ghanaians for a drink after the meeting and that they had already arrived, waiting, seated just outside the meeting room. There had been general agreement earlier in the mission that Ghanaian counterparts could be invited to social occasions and evening meetings from time to time in order to reduce the "threat" of the mission team's appraisal. Dupre, though, was from a rather formal French organizational background, and Mathuri was extremely concerned about the status and prestige of the IDB mission vis-à-vis the Ghanaian government. Consequently, they were both annoyed by the fact that Eduardo had chosen this evening to invite local people to the hotel and were disturbed by their early arrival.

Eduardo, on the other hand, had offered the invitation to the Ghanaians rather spontaneously and, assuming the meeting would not be long, had suggested they wait outside the meeting room until they could all go have a drink together in the bar. The two Ghanaians, Peter Ewe and Kwame Awakopoware, were not aware that the meeting had been called to discuss interpersonal relations within the team and were laughing and joking with Eduardo and Aziz outside the meeting room.

Gradually all the team members drifted into the meeting room and Bjørn, who walked in last, immediately sensed the tense atmosphere.

He had seen the Ghanaians outside and wondered what they were doing there. As he sat down, Bernard and Raj both exploded, saying that everyone had been placed in a most difficult situation, not only by Eduardo's invitation to the Ghanaians, but also by Bjørn who had called a meeting to waste time talking about the way the team worked together when everyone should have been preparing for the project work of the next day.

Questions for Discussion

1. What were the motivation profiles of each of the mission team members in terms of *high, medium,* and *low?*

Bjørn Sorgenfeldt	n(Ach) _____	n(Aff) _____	n(Pow) _____
Eduardo Caballero	n(Ach) _____	n(Aff) _____	n(Pow) _____
Aziz Tanod	n(Ach) _____	n(Aff) _____	n(Pow) _____
Bernard Dupre	n(Ach) _____	n(Aff) _____	n(Pow) _____
Raj Mathuri	n(Ach) _____	n(Aff) _____	n(Pow) _____
John Anderson	n(Ach) _____	n(Aff) _____	n(Pow) _____

2. What conflict was created by role requirements? What conflict was created by differing cultural assumptions and values? What conflict was created by differing motivational factors? To what degree are they interrelated?

3. If you were Bjørn, how would you handle the meeting?

Exercise G. A self-assessment exercise on *basic value orientations*[8] is presented to the members of the group who spontaneously select the item of each pair they agree most with:

1. Wars are unavoidable.
2. Wars are avoidable.

3. Bad luck is conditioned by our behaviour.
4. Bad luck is something we do not control.

5. To keep trying is the key to success.
6. Success comes and goes according to circumstances.

7. People's failure is due to uncontrolled events.
8. People fail because they do not use the right approaches to cope with problems.

---

[8]Developed by P. Casse using J.B. Rotter's theory.

9. Promotions are linked to good work.
10. To take advantage of opportunities is the key to promotions.

11. Whatever you do some people will never like you.
12. People will like you if you approach them the right way.

13. Our personality is determined by our genes.
14. Our personality is a function of what we decide to become.

15. The art of living is to have faith in one's own destiny.
16. To live happily is to assume responsibility for one's own destiny.

17. Good planning leads to success.
18. Fate determines success.

19. Life can be unfair to some people.
20. Some people just don't handle life the right way.

21. Things can be modified according to our deeds.
22. What has to happen happens.

23. To be at the right place at the right time is critical in life.
24. To be alert and ready to take initiatives is critical in life.

25. Adversity is something we fight against.
26. Adversity is something we adapt to.

27. Power is in the hands of a minority of people who control our society.
28. Each individual is accountable for what happens in our society.

29. One can find strengths in each individual.
30. There are people who are simply hopeless.

31. Most rational decisions are effective in controlling situations.
32. To decide at random is by and large as effective as any systematic decision-making process.

33. Our survival depends on forces that we are not aware of.
34. Our survival depends on our ability to understand and control the world.

35. One should be able to learn from one's own mistakes.
36. Mistakes do not help some things and situations change so rapidly.

37. Many failures are due to unforseen events.
38. Failures are mostly due to ignorance.

39. Hard work helps people make things happen to them.
40. Chance plays an important role in people's lives.

SCORING

Put a check next to the selected numbers and add them up.

Internal Orientation	External Orientation
2 _____	1 _____
3 _____	4 _____
5 _____	6 _____
8 _____	7 _____
9 _____	10 _____
12 _____	11 _____
14 _____	13 _____
16 _____	15 _____
17 _____	18 _____
20 _____	19 _____
21 _____	22 _____
24 _____	23 _____
25 _____	26 _____
28 _____	27 _____
29 _____	30 _____
31 _____	32 _____
34 _____	33 _____
35 _____	36 _____
38 _____	37 _____
39 _____	40 _____
TOTAL: _____	TOTAL: _____

Participants are given a brief explanation regarding Rotter's theory when they have finalized their scoring.

According to J.B. Rotter
"people differ in the tendency to attribute satisfactions and failures to themselves rather than to external causes."

Internal people (I score) believe that reward comes from one's own behavior; that they can control themselves and their destinies.

External people (E score) believe that reward comes from external sources; that their fates are in the hands of powerful forces.

A short discussion on the intercultural implications of the theory follows the trainer's presentation. Then the group is asked to identify the dominant orientation of the North American culture (basically internal) and that of the Latin American culture (basically external). Two groups are set up. One works on the characteristics typical of the US and the other on the main cultural traits of the Latin American culture using the 40 items of the self-assessment exercise for reflection.

An illustration of that process is provided hereunder:

US CULTURE	LATIN AMERICAN CULTURE
• People's misfortunes result from the mistakes they make.	• Many unhappy things in people's lives are presently due to bad luck.
• Becoming a success is a matter of hard work; luck has little or nothing to do with it.	• Getting a good job depends mainly on being in the right place at the right time.
• When I make plans, I am almost certain that I can make them work.	• It is not always wise to plan too far ahead because many things turn out to be a matter of good or bad fortune anyhow.
• There is some good in everybody.	• There are certain people who are just no good.
• Most misfortunes are the result of lack of ability, ignorance, laziness, or all three.	• In the long run the best things that happen to us are balanced by the good ones.

Exercise H. Finally the "Persona" exercise is proposed to the group. It goes like this:

Phase 1. Each participant reads the twelve following *"persona identifications"* and decides on the one which is the closest to what he or she thinks he or she is. (30 minutes)

PERSONA IDENTIFICATION

TYPE 1

At work, do you perceive yourself as:

(1) a natural promoter

(2) disliking routine jobs

(3) operating through hunches

(4) being creative and full of new ideas (imaginative)

(5) careless with details

(6) status-oriented (you like to feel important and needed)

(7) very loyal and hard-working if you feel that your work is properly appreciated

(8) a natural leader

(9) someone who does not take criticism too well

(10) self-demanding

(11) full of energy and impulsive

(12) action-oriented

(13) sometimes impertinent

(14) good at taking orders from people you feel are superior to you

(15) always looking for new projects

(16) independent

(17) making quick decisions (sometimes too quick)

(18) restless when there is a lack of challenge

(19) an achiever

(20) liking success very much

PERSONA IDENTIFICATION

TYPE 2

At work, do you perceive yourself as:

(1) dependable and trustworthy

(2) being factual, practical and down-to-earth

(3) hating making decisions in a hurry

(4) good at holding the center together

(5) a determined person (you know what you want)

(6) aiming for perfection

(7) pacing yourself

(8) reliable

 (9) taking orders without resentment

(10) tactful and diplomatic

(11) respectful for authority

(12) a builder, an organizer

(13) patient and cool

(14) stubborn at times

(15) business-oriented

(16) perseverant

(17) always preparing, planning for the future

(18) having a distaste for ignorance

(19) an organizational person

(20) liking the familiar

PERSONA IDENTIFICATION
TYPE 3

At work, do you perceive yourself as:

 (1) thinking and talking fast

 (2) good at Public Relations

 (3) being able to meet a crisis swiftly

 (4) original

 (5) unpredictable

 (6) having a flashing intellect

 (7) good at playing with abstract ideas

 (8) being reluctant to work overtime

 (9) impatient with slow listeners

(10) being perceived as too progressive

(11) making instant decisions and going into action on the spot

(12) refusing to fit into stale patterns

(13) enjoying arguments

(14) witty

(15) ready to try anything once

(16) absent-minded at times

(17) persuasive

(18) changing your mind about things and people

(19) starting action on the grounds of a single hint

(20) being more a "consultant" than an organization person

PERSONA IDENTIFICATION
TYPE 4

At work, do you perceive yourself as:

(1) dependable

(2) sometimes feeling inadequate

(3) tenacious

(4) being deeply attached to your organization

(5) resenting drastic changes which have not been thought through

(6) having a need for being understood (responsive to kindness)

(7) preferring to lead than to be led

(8) loyal

(9) money-oriented

(10) an industrious employee

(11) mixing family and work in various ways

(12) taking your work seriously

(13) full of sensitive insight into human nature

(14) having a sense of humor

(15) always ready to help

(16) feeling things

(17) withdrawing when a crisis occurs

(18) seldom revealing your true inner thoughts

(19) enjoying working lunches

(20) moody

PERSONA IDENTIFICATION
TYPE 5

At work, do you perceive yourself as:

(1) liking titles

(2) fully equipped to take charge

(3) open to others' ideas

(4) good at focusing upon the essentials

(5) being able to turn a failure into victory overnight

(6) not interested too much in figures and statistics

(7) enjoying being involved in big projects

(8) liking compliments as well as feedback on your performance

(9) having an unbelievable vitality

(10) disliking to work behind the scenes

(11) ambitious

(12) having a strong sense of responsibility

(13) being sensitive about your rights

(14) someone who cannot stand to be underestimated

(15) good at handing out free advice

(16) sensitive to the working environment that has to be cozy

(17) hating office intrigues

(18) courageous

(19) always interested in what is going on in the office

(20) feeling useless when not assuming some kind of obligation

PERSONA IDENTIFICATION
TYPE 6

At work, do you perceive yourself as:

(1) sensitive to fairness

(2) giving service without seeking reward

(3) having a strong analytical ability

(4) liking to use a step-by-step approach

(5) sometimes being tense at work

(6) perfectionist

(7) excellent critic

(8) being blunt in pointing out mistakes and flaws

(9) having a perfect eye for details

(10) versatile

(11) never turning in sloppy work

(12) having a strong sense of ethics

(13) liking to work quietly alone

(14) having a sharp sense of discrimination

(15) precise

(16) catching your own mistakes

(17) enjoying regular schedules

(18) disliking noise and confusion when working

(19) plain-spoken

(20) resenting too close supervision

PERSONA IDENTIFICATION
TYPE 7

At work, do you perceive yourself as:

(1) having a profound sense of justice

(2) being a peacemaker

(3) sometimes inconsistent

(4) having a lot of ups and downs

(5) being very sensitive to the harmony (or lack thereof) in the working environment

(6) good at clearing the air of disagreements

(7) enjoying probing

(8) always trying to understand the pros and cons of a situation

(9) logical (sometimes for the sake of the logic itself)

(10) creating tensions all around

(11) believing that intelligent argument is entertainment

(12) good at seeing others' points of view

(13) enjoying teasing

(14) avoiding confrontations

(15) weighing everything on all sides

(16) having some trouble at times in making up your mind

(17) unpredictable

(18) being involved in many things without talking about it

(19) having a certain "charm"

(20) impartial

PERSONA IDENTIFICATION
TYPE 8

At work, do you perceive yourself as:

(1) a self-contained person

(2) having a strong inner confidence

(3) having a master plan for the future

(4) "impressing" people all around

(5) self-motivated

(6) a very resourceful person

(7) sure of yourself

(8) blaming yourself for your own mistakes (being harsh on yourself sometimes)

(9) a self-controlled person

(10) fearless

(11) accepting the inevitable with grace, if the stakes are high enough

(12) cool-headed

(13) knowing the price of success

(14) loyal to the people who pay you (the ultimate loyalty is to yourself)

(15) having long memories

(16) intense and tenacious

(17) being serious about your career

(18) committed to your own code and ideas

(19) never losing sight of your ultimate goal

(20) passionate

PERSONA IDENTIFICATION
TYPE 9

At work, do you perceive yourself as:

(1) oriented to the present

(2) cheerful and willing to help

(3) enthusiastic and optimistic

(4) never doing things halfway (fairly speedy)

(5) casual

(6) taking initiative and bold

(7) making forthright statements

(8) curious, wanting to know the "whys"

(9) charming

(10) talking about your own talents and abilities without any hesitation

(11) ready to promise to deliver almost anything

(12) not strong on follow-through

(13) right more often than wrong (lucky)

(14) sensitive about your integrity

(15) having occasional outbursts of temper

(16) enjoying travel

(17) having non-lasting angers

(18) a dreamer

(19) being happy with yourself in general

(20) someone who does not complain lightly

PERSONA IDENTIFICATION
TYPE 10

At work, do you perceive yourself as:

(1) reserved (people sometimes think that you are shy)

(2) the person who is called upon when there is trouble

(3) conservative

(4) well-organized

(5) minding your own business

(6) coldly determined to get where you are going

(7) dislike being pushed around

(8) conscientious

(9) feeling miserable if you make mistakes

(10) realistic, serious, solid

(11) searching for the real position of power (not fancy titles)

(12) impatient with methods that are not sound or procedures that lack common sense

(13) efficient

(14) good at figures and statistics

(15) a hard worker

(16) balancing your family life with business

(17) good at documenting what you argue for

(18) formal

(19) good at listening to other people

(20) avoiding wasting your time

PERSONA IDENTIFICATION
TYPE 11

At work, do you perceive yourself as:

(1) liking to make new friends (sometimes giving more friendship than receiving it)

(2) full of original ideas

(3) making an instant and lasting impression on people

(4) future-oriented

(5) leaving others breathless sometimes

(6) ingenious and interested in many different fields

(7) sometimes being considered as irrational and impractical

(8) inventive, with intuitive powers

(9) odd in your habits

(10) a thinker

(11) someone without driving ambition

(12) being unable to stick to regular schedules

(13) disliking making decisions

(14) reluctant to give orders

(15) absent-minded and forgetful

(16) tolerant

(17) looking for changes

(18) liking to experiment

(19) patient

(20) losing yourself in deep thought (retreating)

PERSONA IDENTIFICATION
TYPE 12

At work, do you perceive yourself as:

 (1) being low-key

 (2) generous

 (3) good at practicing empathy

 (4) more receptive than active

 (5) observing what is going on in the working environment

 (6) being very careful in revealing what your true aims are

 (7) disguising your motives (it is your own business)

 (8) sometimes appearing inconsistent

 (9) imaginative (given to daydreaming)

(10) understanding human suffering

(11) disliking doing something which offends your sensitivity

(12) not being understood

(13) withdrawing when unhappy

(14) preferring abrupt change to lengthy explanation

(15) good at teaching or training (coaching)

(16) ultra-sensitive about others' moods

(17) avoiding being embarrassed in front of other people

(18) not looking for extra responsibilities

(19) lonely

(20) preferring not to tell things like they are if there is a risk of shocking people

Phase 2. The members of the group adjust their selected profile by deleting the definitions or items they do not like (those which they are), borrowing from other persona identifications things they believe they feel are missing.

Phase 3. When they are ready, people who share more or less the same profile meet and discuss them (What do we have in common?).

Phase 4. Participants with different profiles meet and talk about the positive and less positive aspects of their eventual interactions.

Phase 5. All the members of the group are asked to describe a culture (fictitious one) which would be completely opposite to their "persona identification." They study their potential relations with such a culture keeping in mind that: most individuals start to question the meaning of their work and their lives when the differences between the persona and the cultural environment are too important.

Issues and Questions:

1. Can the participants relate the 12 descriptions with some existing cultures?

2. What about the interactions between people with different personas?

3. How should a multicultural manager handle each persona?

Exercise I. The following case study is analyzed by the group:

CASE STUDY:

Understanding one's own organization[9]

The organization, a bank, had been established for a long time and functioned remarkably smoothly, if not always very effficiently. It made almost 100 large loans per year, and prepared about 100 voluminous sector and policy reports per year for the authorities and for its clients. The intellectual quality of these reports was widely recognized. To maintain and further enhance that quality, a committee of the vice-president and all department heads (almost 20) met twice a week, all the year around, to review, on average, two reports per three hour sessions. Department heads had, of course, no time to read and edit all these reports, and relied on their staff to do it. For this purpose, rosters of about 30 reliable staff (i.e. staff with more than one year in the

---

[9]Created by Mr. R.H. Springuel of the Economic Development Institute of the World Bank.

institution but not yet at a managerial position) were constituted in each department. Whenever a report reached a department, a secretary picked the next staff on the roster (alphabetical order) and sent him the report to review and write a short note for the director, within 24 hours of receipt of the report. The note addressed two questions: (1) Is this report departing from the usual bank policies and procedures? and, (2) Is this report of particular interest to this department?

The staff member who received the report with these questions dropped everything he did and worked like mad to meet the deadline. Two days later he went to the committee with his director, sat in the back and listened to the use (or lack of use) his director made of his note, and to all the remarks made by other directors. He could easily spot all the points he had missed, the conclusions reached and their reasons. Each mid-level staff attended such meetings about once every two months. Shortly after his arrival, a new chief executive decided that this procedure was becoming too time consuming and divided the committee into five smaller ones. This stopped the need for bank-wide circulation of reports and for review by mid-level staff. About five years later, staff started complaining that they did not know what was going on, and managers, that the new staff did not learn the policies as well as they themselves did when they joined.

Question: Identify the motivation factors involved in the case. Pinpoint at least 5 cultural traits within the case.

5. Time: Two or three days.

6. Conceptual Framework:

INPUT 1

The Maslow Need Hierarchy[10]

Abraham Maslow theorized that experienced needs are the primary influences on an individual's behavior. When a particular need emerges, it determines the individual's behavior in terms of motivations, priorities, and action taken. Thus motivated behavior is the result of the tension—either pleasant or unpleasant—experienced when a need presents itself. The goal of the behavior is the reduction of

---

[10]Reprinted from: J.W. Pfeiffer and J.E. Jones (Eds.), *The 1972 Annual Handbook for Group Facilitators*. San Diego, CA: University Associates, 1972. Used with permission.

this tension or discomfort and the behavior, itself, will be appropriate for facilitating the satisfaction of the need. Only unsatisfied needs are prime sources of motivation.

Understanding behaviors and their goals involves gaining insight into presently unsatisfied needs. Maslow developed a method for gaining insight by providing categories of needs in a hierarchical structure. He placed all human needs, from primitive or immature (in terms of the behaviors they foster) to civilized or mature needs, into five need systems. He believed that there is a natural process whereby individuals fulfilled needs in ascending order from most immature to most mature. This progression through the need hierarchy is seen as the climbing of a ladder where the individual must have experienced secure footing on the first rung in order to experience the need to step up to the next higher rung. The awareness of the need to climb further up the ladder is a function of having fulfilled the need of managing the preceding rung, and only satisfactory fulfillment of this need will allow the individual to deal with the new need or rung. Inability to fulfill a lower-order need or difficulty in fulfilling a lower-order need may result in an individual's locking in on immature behavior patterns or may produce a tendency to return to immature behaviors under stress any time an individual feels a lower-order need not fulfilled to his satisfaction. The individual may also revert to behaviors which fulfilled lower-order needs when the satisfaction of higher needs are temporarily blocked. That is not to say that any need is ever completely satisfied; rather, Maslow indicates that there must be at least partial fulfillment before an individual can become aware of the tensions manifested by a higher-order need and have the freedom to pursue its fulfillment.

The basic level represents needs which reflect physiological and survival goals. At this level are such factors as shelter, clothing, food, sex, and other necessities. In a culture like the North American one where these basic needs are almost automatically met, there is not likely to be any need tension concerning the fulfillment of Basic needs. However, individuals adapt this basic level upward to include such needs as avoidance of physical discomfort, pleasant working environment, or more money for providing creature comforts.

The second level of the hierarchy consists of Safety needs. When the individual has at least partially fulfilled the Basic needs, he will experience the tensions relating to needs of security, orderliness, protective rules, and general risk avoidance. These needs are often satisfied by an adequate salary, insurance policies, a good burglar alarm system for his business, a doorman for his apartment building, etc.

When Safety needs have been met, the individual will become less preoccupied with self and will endeavor to form interpersonal relationships. The relative success of this need for Belongingness will result in his feeling accepted and appreciated by others. Thus the third level needs concern family ties, friendship and group membership.

When an individual feels secure in his relationships with others, he will probably seek to gain special status within the group. His need tension will be associated with ambition and a desire to excel. These Ego-Status needs will motivate the individual to seek out opportunities to display his competence in an effort to gain social and professional rewards.

Because Ego-Status fulfillment is greatly dependent upon the ability of others to respond appropriately to the individual's efforts to perform in a superior way, they are the most difficult to fulfill satisfactorily. However, if the individual has gained satisfaction on level four, he may be able to move up to level five—Self-Actualization. At this level, the individual is concerned with personal growth and may fulfill this need by challenging himself to become more creative, demanding greater achievement of himself, and, in general, directing himself to measure up to his own criteria of personal success. Self-Actualizing behaviors must include risk-taking, seeking autonomy, and developing freedom to act.

INPUT 2

Herzberg's Theory on the Satisfiers and Dissatisfiers[11]

Herzberg analyzed and classified the job *content* factors or satisfying experiences as follows:

Satisfiers

- Achievement
- Recognition
- Work itself
- Responsibility
- Advancement
- Growth

He categorized the *context* or environmental factors causing dissatisfaction to include:

Dissatisfiers

- Company policy and administration
- Supervision

---

[11]National Industrial Conference Board. *Behavioral Scientists: Their Theories and their Work.*

- Working conditions
- Interpersonal relations (with superiors, subordinates, and peers)
- Salary
- Status
- Job security
- Personal life

Definition of Factors

These satisfying and dissatisfying factors may generally be called categorizations or interpretations of actual experiences reported by the respondents. For clarification, Herzberg gives examples of real experiences as they fit into the categories:

Achievement—Achievement refers to the personal satisfaction of completing a job, solving problems, seeing the results of one's efforts.

Recognition—As a satisfier, recognition is in terms of a *job* well done or personal accomplishment, as contrasted with general recognition in a "human relations" sense, which is categorized under interpersonal relations.

Work Itself—The actual content of the job and its positive or negative effect upon the employee is a central feature of the analysis, whether the job be characterized as interesting or boring, varied or routine, creative or stultifying, excessively easy or excessively difficult, challenging or nondemanding.

Responsibility—Both responsibility and authority in relation to the job are included here. Specifically, "responsibility" refers to the employee's control over his own job, or to his being given responsibility for the work of others. This factor is different from the consideration of whether or not there is a gap between a person's authority and the authority he needs to carry out his job responsibilities. When this gap was reported, Herzberg classified it under "company policy and administration," on the assumption that the discrepancy was evidence of poor management.

Advancement—Responses grouped under advancement are restricted to actual change upward in status. In cases where a transfer or job change involves increased opportunity for responsibility, but with no accompanying change in status, the responses were grouped under "responsibility."

Growth—Responses under "growth" include actual learning of new skills, with greater possibility of advancement within the current occupational speciality or in others, as well as possible growth. In the "possible" growth column Herzberg listed responses not only indicating immediate growth in the job (e.g., a craftsman becoming a draftsman), but possibilities for future growth as a result of the immediate growth (e.g., the same craftsman's move to draftsman may open the door to his eventually becoming a design engineer). In the same line of reasoning, "negative" possibilities of growth were weighed (e.g., lack of formal education as a barrier to future growth).

Company Policy and Administration—Experiences relating to some over all aspect of the company (as contrasted with supervisor-subordinate relations) were listed in the category. Those include responses reflecting feelings about the adequacy or inadequacy of company organization and management: for example, lines of communication so confused that an employee does not know for whom he is actually working; or is not given adequate authority to complete his task, etc.

Supervision—Generally this category refers only to the competency or technical ability of supervision, as contrasted with interpersonal relations. Factors listed under "supervision" include: the supervisor's willingness or unwillingness to teach or to delegate responsibility, fairness versus unfairness, and the supervisor's knowledge of his job.

Working Conditions—These responses have to do with the physical environment of the job, including the amount of work, the facilities for performing it, light, temperature, tools, space, and ventilation, and the general appearance of the work place.

Interpersonal Relations—Herzberg broke down responses in this category into relations involving the respondent and his superiors, subordinates, and peers. He concedes that interpersonal relations play a role in almost all of the major categories, for example, in company policy and administration, personal recognition, and change in status; but responses listed under "interpersonal relations" were only described by the respondent as being an *explicit* interaction between himself and someone else in the firm. Implicit factors were listed elsewhere.

A further breakdown of the responses was made in terms of the nature of the interpersonal interaction. On the one hand, there are the "sociotechnical" interactions, which involve interaction in the performance of the job. On the other hand, there are interactions that take place during working hours and between others in the company, but which are called purely social interaction—coffee breaks, lunches, and recreation.

Salary—This catetory includes all responses involving compensation. Virtually all the responses center on wage or salary increases or unfilled expectation of increases.

Status—Status, as a category, was restricted to responses involving some indication of status *per se* as a factor in the respondent's feeling about the job and mentioned specifically. For example, included here were such responses as: having a carpeted office, having a secretary, driving a company car, having access to private "upper echelon" dining facilities. Change in *actual* status—promotion, advancement—were categorized under "advancement," in which status and recognition are implicit. However, inferred status was not listed in this category; only those responses in which some appurtenance of status was mentioned were listed.

Job Security—The criterion for this category is *objective* signs of the presence or absence of job security, *not feelings of security*. Responses under job security include tenure and company stability or instability.

Personal Life—Factors in the respondent's personal life which affect the job were excluded from this category. Only those job factors that affect personal life were included, so long as these factors had an influence on the way the respondent felt about the job. For example, a response about the company's moving an employee to a location where he or his family were unhappy fell into this category.

Categorization of Factors

Clearly, not every respondent's answers fell neatly into the two columns of "satisfiers" or "dissatisfiers." There was some overlap or extension of a "satisfier" into the "dissatisfier" column in some instances. However, in analyzing and categorizing the responses, Herzberg listed a total of sixteen factors which were mentioned with enough frequency to differentiate statistically between the general "satisfier" or "dissatisfier" categories.

Herzberg called the dissatisfiers *hygiene* factors, borrowing the medical and paramedical definition of hygiene as "preventive and environmental." They are also sometimes referred to as "maintenance" factors.

The satisfiers, which are all related to the job itself, were called *motivators,* since other findings in the studies suggest that they are effective in motivating the employee to greater performance and productivity.

In establishing his motivation-hygiene theory, Herzberg draws heavily upon the hierarchy of needs developed by Maslow. Herzberg stresses that the factors which truly motivate the work are "growth" factors, or those that give the worker a sense of personal accomplishment through the challenge of the job itself. Real motivation is seen as resulting from the worker's involvement in accomplishing an interesting task and from his feeling of accomplishment alone, and not from the working conditions or environmental factors that are peripheral to the job. Clearly, there is a connection here with Maslow's theory of self-actualization, which states that the motivated person receives satisfaction from the sheer love of doing the job.

Deficit Needs and Management Practices

The dissatisfiers may be classed as "deficit" needs (their importance is felt only in their absence). Herzberg found, for example, that good working conditions (physical environment, congenial co-workers, good supervision) were rarely named as contributing to job satisfaction. On the other hand, bad working conditions were frequently named as sources of dissatisfaction.

Even more significant in Herzberg's model of worker motivation is the contention that the satisfiers and dissatisfiers are separate, distinct, discrete factors, rather than opposite poles of the same factor. As he expresses it, the fact that something doesn't dissatisfy doesn't mean that it satisfies.

He says that most of industry's attempts to motivate workers, or to establish a climate in which workers will be self-motivated, have taken the form of stressing hygiene factors while ignoring the motivators. As an example, he cites so-called fringe benefits. People are dissatisfied if fringe benefits are missing or inadequate, says Herzberg, but their existence is worth nothing in terms of getting real motivation from people. So fringe benefits are relegated to the status of dissatisfiers, since their importance is felt only in their absence.

Self-Actualization Through Meaningful Work

Again, using Maslow's hierarchy of needs as one basis for his views, Herzberg insists that the hygiene factors are important and that they, like Maslow's lower level needs, must be adequately provided if a person is to rise above them to the self-actualizing concerns of involving himself in meaningful tasks. If the hygiene factors are removed or diminished, the worker slips down a level or two in the hierarchy and becomes concerned about them, instead of about the content of his work. One gauge of the health of an organization, in this context, is not the complete absence of complaints or disgruntlement, but the nature of the complaints. If a man is unhappy because he doesn't have a carpet in his office, he is at an entirely different level of mental health than the man who complains that his job is boring, according to Herzberg.

If, as Herzberg claims, industry has expended a great deal of time, money, and effort trying to gain worker motivation the wrong way, should these hygiene factors be stopped or reduced? Herzberg says "no," for they will still be an important part of the worker's needs and demands and, he conjectures, even more of such things as fringe benefits will be needed because "everyone else has them" and the economic needs of people still must be met. But, according to Herzberg, management is fooling itself if it expects to get motivated workers in return. "Longer vacations don't motivate."

INPUT 3

Managers and Motivation Theories[12]

Five basic assumptions are pointed out in one way or another by six behavioral scientists or management specialists (C. Argyris, P. Drucker, F. Herzberg, R. Likert, A. Maslow, D. McGregor):

Assumption 1: Most employees have a desire to use a significant portion of their skills and abilities at work.

Assumption 2: Most organizations do a relatively poor job of offering their employees opportunities to use their skills and abilities.

Assumption 3: Failure to utilize talents and skills often makes work a less satisfying experience than it could otherwise be.

Assumption 4: This same failure makes the organization less economically effective than it could otherwise be.

Assumption 5: Management's challenge, therefore, is to structure the work experience in such a way that both employees' needs for satisfaction, through use of their abilities, and the organization's need to be economically effective, are met.

INPUT 4

A New Approach to Motivation

A. According to C.G. Jung people have four basic needs:

Figure 24. Jung's Four Basic Needs

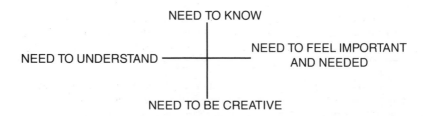

NEED TO KNOW

NEED TO UNDERSTAND ——————— NEED TO FEEL IMPORTANT AND NEEDED

NEED TO BE CREATIVE

---

[12]D.A. Whitsett, "Making Sense of Management Theories," *Personnel,* May-June 1975.

B. An effective manager will appeal to the four needs as follows:

- Appeal to the senses (need to know)

- Appeal to the intellect (need to understand)

- Appeal to the imagination (need to be creative)

- Appeal to the emotions (need to feel important and needed)

7. Handouts and Readings:

(a) Handouts

Caspe, M.S., "Motivating People to Perform on Design and Construction Projects," *Project Management Quarterly*, December 1979, pp. 34-38.

Clausen, A.W., "Listening and Responding to Employees' Concerns," *Harvard Business Review*, January-February 1980.

Cooper, M.R., Morgan, B.S., Foley, P.M., Kaplan, L.B., "Changing Employee Values: Deepening Discontent?," *Harvard Business Review*, January-February 1979.

Hall, J., "To Achieve or Not: The Manager's Choice," *California Management Review*, Vol. XVII, No. 4, Summer 1976.

Herzberg, F., "Motivation—Hygiene Profiles: Pinpointing What Aids the Organization," *Organizational Dynamics*, Fall 1974.

Herzberg, F., "One More Time: How do you Motivate Employees?," *Harvard Business Review*, January - February 1968.

Herzberg, F., Paul, W.D., and Robertson, K.B., "Enrichment Pays Off," *Harvard Business Review*, March - April 1969.

Katz, D., "The Motivational Basis of Organizational Behavior," *Behavioral Science*, Vol. 9, 1964, pp. 131-46.

Likert, R., "Motivational Approach to Management Development," *Harvard Business Review*, July - August 1959.

Litwin, G.H., and Siebrecht A., "Integrators and Entrepreneurs: Their Motivation and Effect on Management," *Hospital Progress*, September 1967.

Magnus, M., "Employee Recognition: A Key to Motivation," *Personnel Journal*, February 1981, pp. 103-107.

McClelland, D.C., "Achievement Motivation Can Be Developed," *Harvard Business Review*, November-December 1965.

McClelland, D.C., "Business Drive and National Achievement," *Harvard Business Review,* July - August 1962.

McClelland, D.C., and Burnham, D., "Power is the Greatest Motivator," *Harvard Business Review,* March - April 1976.

Reilly, A.J., "Human Needs and Behavior," *The 1975 Annual Handbook for Group Facilitators,* pp. 123-125.

Richum, S., "Motivation: The Art of Building a Winning Team," *Leadership,* May 1979, pp. 25-29.

Roche, W.J., and MacKinnon, N.L., "Motivating People with Meaningful Work," *Harvard Business Review,* May - June 1970.

Rotter, J.B., "External Control and Internal Control," *Psychology Today,* June 1971.

Whitsett, D.A., "Where are Your Unenriched Jobs?," *Harvard Business Review,* January - February 1975.

Yorks, L., "Determining Job Enrichment Feasibility," *Personnel,* November - December 1974.

Yorks, L., "Key Elements in Implementing Job Enrichment," *Personnel,* September - October 1973.

(b) Readings

Argyris, C., *Integrating the Individual and the Organization.* New York: Wiley, 1964.

de Charms, R., *Personal Causation.* New York: Academic Press, 1968.

Gellerman, S.W., *Management by Motivations.* New York: AMA, 1968.

Herzberg, F., *The Motivation to Work.* New York: Wiley, 1959.

Herzberg, F., *Work and the Nature of Man.* New York: A Mentor Book, 1975.

Jaques, E., *Work, Creativity and Social Justice.* New York: International Universities Press, 1970.

Lawler, E.E., *Motivation in Work Organization.* Belmont, California: Brooks/Cole, 1973.

Levinson, H., *Psychological Man.* Cambridge, MA: The Levinson Institute, Inc., 1976.

Likert, R., *The Human Organization.* New York: McGraw-Hill, 1967.

Lippitt, G.L., This, L.E., and Bidwell, R.G., (eds.), "Optimizing Human Resources," Reading, MA: Addison-Wesley, 1971.

Litwin, G., and Stringer, R., *Managing Motivation from Motivation and Organizational Climate*. Cambridge, MA: Harvard Business School.

Maslow, A., *Motivation and Personality*. New York: Harper and Brothers, 1954.

McClelland, D., *The Achieving Society*. New York: The MacMillan Company, 1961.

McClelland, D., *Power, The Inner Experience*. New York: Irvington Publishers, 1975.

McClelland, D., and Winter, D.G., *Motivating Economic Achievement*. New York: The Free Press, 1971.

McGregor, D., *The Human Side of Enterprise*. New York: McGraw-Hill, 1960.

McGregor, D., *The Professional Manager*. New York: McGraw-Hill, 1967.

Skinner, B.F., *Beyond Freedom and Dignity*. New York: Knopf, 1971.

Vroom, V.H., *Work and Motivation*. New York: Wiley, 1964.

Vroom, V.H., and Deci, E.L., (eds.), *Management and Motivation*. New York: Penguin Books, 1970.

"Synergy is a creative combination of two elements to produce something new or greater than the sum of its parts (The conception of the human being from egg and sperm is the highest form of synergy)."

A.G. Banet

Workshop 4
Synergistic Teamwork:
Seven plus nine makes twenty?

---

1. Introduction: A group is not automatically a team, but a team is always a group. What is the difference? The difference stems from the fact that in a team, internal and external resources are tapped in such a systematic way that the group objectives (i.e. what people want or have to achieve or accomplish) are reached in the best possible way.

Team building is the process by which a group tries to maximize the use of its resources so that it is able to achieve its goals at the best cost (psychological, economical, social, cultural…).

The main implication of team building is that a team is not always productive and efficient. It has been shown again and again that to bring bright people with different cultural backgrounds together to work on a project is not always a guarantee of success. Bright people can constitute "lousy" teams! The synergistic process also has to be organized and managed. If synergy is the process by which team members are able to go beyond what they are used to being and doing and produce something new, unique and far superior to what each individual can create, then the role of a multicultural manager is to make sure that the confrontation of cultural differences among the members of his or her team will be synergistic. Let's face it, seven plus nine can make twenty; it can also make three!

2. Aim: To demonstrate that cross-cultural interactions can be synergistic if well managed.

3. Objectives: Participants will:

(a) understand what an intercultural team is about (group discussion and conceptual framework: Input 1);

(b) observe the dynamics of an intercultural team confronted with a simple task (exercise);

(c) experience and analyze the synergistic team process (exercise and conceptual framework: Input 2);

(d) apply the "TAO" approach to synergistic team building (interpersonal interactions and group discussion);

(e) examine the challenges of a multicultural manager who has to lead a team made up of people from different cultures (exercise and group discussion);

(f) practice three "creativity" methods applied to intercultural issues (exercises).

4. Process:

Exercise A. What is an intercultural team? Each participat writes a definition on a piece of cardboard (one sentence).

• Participants then meet in trios and try to accommodate their definitions so that they can agree on one common formulation (without voting);

• The trios share their definitions and the group aims at reaching a consensus on one text;

• The entire group compares the definition it has invented with this statement:

> "A cross-cultural team is a group made up of people having different values, beliefs, and assumptions, who try to achieve a set of common objectives (chosen by the group or imposed upon it) in the best possible way."

Exercise B. The following exercise is given to the group to demonstrate the meaning of *Synergistic Teamwork*.

Phase 1: The trainer reads, slowly and aloud a list of fifty words selected at random.

Phase 2: The participants listen carefully to the words without taking any notes.

Phase 3: The trainer asks the group members to write down individually as many words as they can remember. When everybody has finished, he/she checks the number of words which have been recorded by the participants. The number of words will generally vary between 8 and 25.

Phase 4: Participants meet in pairs and come up with joint lists of words. Each pair will have a list of more than 25 words.

Phase 5 and 6: Same as Phase 4, but this time the people meet in groups of four and eight. The scores will be superior to 32 words for the groups of four and superior to 40 words for the groups of eight.

Phase 7: The trainer asks anyone of the participants to list as many words as possible on an individual basis. It is amazing to see how well everybody does compared with the first phase.

An analysis of the various steps leads to the following conclusions:

(1) Teamwork is more effective than individual work (the score of a team is at least as good as the score of its best member);

(2) Teamwork motivates, sustains the participants' attention and reinforces creativity;

(3) Teamwork (when well organized or managed) gives an opportunity to people to improve their individual performance.

Exercise C. A small group (between 6 and 12 people) of volunteers sit in the middle of the room while the rest of the participants observe the exercise. The following instructions are given to the volunteers.

Instructions for the Volunteers

Your ship has just sunk and your group is safe on a raft which means that you have a good chance to survive. There is still room for *three* people. Please (a) make a choice among the list hereunder of the three individuals you are going to take on board, (b) decide on how you will prevent the others from climbing on the raft and jeopardizing everybody's life.

You have 30 minutes to accomplish the given task.

List of people in the water.

1. *Five people that you know nothing about*

   - A child (about 10 years old)
   - A man (in his thirties)
   - A wounded woman
   - A couple of elderly people

2. *Five people that you recognize as being*

   - A doctor
   - An officer
   - A pastor
   - A couple of newlyweds

The observers receive both the volunteers' instructions as well as the following ones:

Instructions for the Observers

Please identify:

(1) The *main* values expressed by the team members when trying to reach a decision;

(2) The *assumptions* (things which are taken for granted) expressed by the participants;

(3) The *decision-making* process experienced by the team.

N.B. Observers do not intervene during the exercise.

After completion of the exercise, a discussion takes place concerning the observers' reactions. Some of the *main values* expressed by the group are related to:

1. saving - a child, a wounded woman, someone who can help and increase the group's chance of survival...(criteria to be used to make a "fair" choice)

2. offering one's own place to somebody else

3. deciding on how to "reject" the non-selected people

4. organizing the group discussion

5. granting the "right" meaning to the exercise

Some of the *main assumptions* are linked to:

1. The overall situation (Are we completely lost? What about help?)

2. The meaning of survival

3. The options available (what about establishing a rotation between the people on the raft and those in the water?)

4. The people in the water (The doctor is a woman!)

5. The objective of the exercise

The decision-making process is mainly characterized by two trends: the *analytical approach,* which is based on an objective understanding of the situation and its potentialities; the *normative* approach with its value orientation.

With the analytical approach, the group decision is based on facts, logic and rational thinking. With the normative approach, the decision is determined by what is perceived as important and less important, feelings, emotions.

Exercise D. The picture below is divided into four spaces which are themselves cut into small pieces according to the pattern presented in Figure 25.

Figure 25.

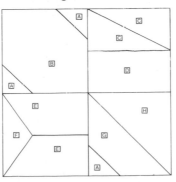

Pieces are put together in a certain order, enclosed in envelopes and given to four volunteers (one per volunteer).

The letters should not appear on the various parts of the picture. They are simply used to determine which pieces fit into which envelope, i.e. Envelope I has pieces A, A, and C; Envelope II has B,C, and E; Envelope III has D, E and B; Envelope IV has F, A and H.

The four volunteers sit around a table (as far away as possible from each other) and open their envelope in which they find the pieces of a square and a set of instructions.

Instructions for the Volunteers

Complete your puzzle (a square) using at least three pieces and respecting the following constraints:

(1) You cannot speak to each other;

(2) Try to finish your puzzle first;

(3) You can give and receive pieces to and from the other volunteers.

The other members of the group watch the various reactions of the volunteers without interfering in the exercise. They receive the following instructions:[1]

Instructions for the Observers

Please observe the team and check the validity of the four following remarks.

When we work in a team:

(1) It is very important for each individual to understand the overall problem which must be solved;

(2) Each individual has to see *how* he or she can contribute towards solving the problem;

---

[1]The video tape recorder can be very effective in this exercise.

(3) There is a need for each individual to be aware of the potential contributions of other individuals;

(4) It is vital to see the other person's problems in order that he or she may be helped to make a maximum contribution.

A group discussion follows the exercise. The trainer conducts the exchange around some key cross-cultural issues:

• Was the objective clear?

• What was the objective?

• Are there different cultural ways to define objectives?

• What about the volunteers' assumptions regarding:

— helping	— leading
— competing	— winning
— sharing	— withdrawing
— giving	— organizing
— receiving	— negotiating

• How did the volunteers communicate? (Did they write?)

• Was there any kind of teamwork during the exercise?

• Others?

Exercise E. Here is a series of 15 skills presented at random. Rank them according to the 11 steps described hereunder.

Step 1: Read the description of the situation and carry out the task.

The situation: You have just been appointed the leader of a team made up of people with different patterns of thinking, feeling and behaving or, to put it differently, who have various assumptions, values and beliefs. It is the first time that you have to manage such a multicultural team.

The task: Rank in order the 15 skills according to their importance in relation to your adjustment as a manager. Use "1" for the most important and "15" for the least important. Do this without talking to anyone (30 minutes). (See Figure 26.)

Figure 26. Skills for Multicultural Managers

To Be Able:	Step 1 Individual Ranking	Step 2 Team Ranking	Step 3 Intercultural Specialists' Ranking	Step 4 Differences Between 1 and 3	Step 5 Differences Between 2 and 3
• To be Persistent					
• To Avoid Attributions					
• To Relate to People					
• To Learn from Interacting					
• To be Able to Communicate					
• To Respect the Other Culture					
• To be Non-Judgmental					
• To Avoid Stereotypes					
• To Practice Empathy					
• To be Aware of One's Own Limitations					
• To be Flexible					
• To be Aware of One's Own Culture					
• To Listen and Observe					
• To Tolerate Ambiguity					
• To Adjust According to People's Reactions					
TOTALS				Individual Score	Team Score

Step 2: Participants meet in teams and reach a consensus on a common ranking. They do not change their individual rankings as determined under Step 1 (45 minutes). (See Figure 26.)

Step 3: The trainer provides the ranking of specialists in the intercultural field[2] (See Figure 27) to be used in Figure 26.

Step 4: The individuals determine their scores by subtracting the specialists' ranking from their rankings (in absolute terms, without taking the minuses and pluses into consideration) and adding up the differences (see Figure 26).

Step 5: The teams determine their scores by subtracting the specialists' ranking from their team ranking (see Figure 26). Add up the differences to find the total team score. Transfer this total team score to step 5 in Figure 28.

Step 6: The average individual scores are calculated as follows: individual scores are added and the total is divided by the number of team members (see Figure 28).

Step 7: The gain scores are identified, i.e., the differences between the team scores and the average individual scores. If the team score is lower than the average individual score than the gain score is positive. If the team score is higher than the individual score, then the gain score is negative (see Figure 28).

Step 8: The lowest score is identified for each team (see Figure 28).

Step 9: The number of scores lower than the team score is recorded for each team (see Figure 28).

Step 10: A discussion takes place regarding the ability of the team to be "synergistic" (see conceptual framework: Input 2):

(a) the higher the gain score the more synergistic the team;

(b) the more individuals' scores that are lower than the team score, the less synergistic the team is.

---

[2]This ranking has been established by about 50 people having strong experience in the intercultural communication field.

Step 11: The participants (a) examine the relevance of the 15 guidelines; (b) criticize the specialists' ranking; (c) create a new "model" for the experts' ranking.

Figure 27. Intercultural Specialists' Ranking

INTERCULTURAL SPECIALISTS' RANKING	RATIONALE
I. Self-Understanding	
1. To be aware of one's own culture	To be aware of the fact that every behavior is influenced by some basic cultural assumptions, values, and beliefs is critical.
2. To be aware of one's own limitations	The awareness should be personalized in the sense that the multicultural manager should know that his or her construction of reality is highly dependent upon the nature and structure of his own pysche.
II. Understanding Others	
3. To practice empathy	The ability to see the world as other people see it is a powerful tool because it has been shown that people prefer to work with managers who give the impression that they understand things from others' viewpoints.
4. To respect the other culture	Tolerance is a *sine qua non* condition for effective cross-cultural interactions. Employees value this kind of attitude from their managers.
5. To learn from interactions	To learn how to learn is a key skill, for each situation is different and requires the manager to adapt.
6. To avoid attributions	To explain other people's behavior using one's own frame of reference leads to misunderstanding and communication breakdowns.
7. To be non-judgmental	To control one's own natural tendency to pass value judgments on other people is also something that the multicultural manager has to learn.
8. To avoid stereotypes	Generalizations lead to misinterpretations and ineffectiveness.

III. Interacting with Others	
9. To be able to communicate	Multicultural managers have to make sure that they communicate effectively. This requires the use of basic skills such as asking open-ended questions, using silence, paraphrasing and reflecting feelings.
10. To relate to people	A multicultural manager must pay special attention to the "maintenance" part of his or her role. Too much energy spent on the task side of the job can jeopardize the entire project.
11. To listen and observe	Listening and observing other people's behavior as well as one's own is highly useful.
12. To be flexible	The multicultural manager must cultivate and expand his or her range of options and choices in order to deal effectively with different situations.
13. To adjust according to people's reactions	He or she must be able to use all the resources available.
IV. General Skills	
14. To tolerate ambiguity	A good tolerance of ambiguity helps the multicultural manager cope with the unavoidable stress of the intercultural setting.
15. To be persistent	To flee and withdraw, while justifiable in the short term, can, in the long term create problems and deadlocks. The multicultural manager must be patient.

Figure 28. Processing of the Teamwork Exercise

	TEAM 1	TEAM 2	TEAM 3	TEAM 4
Step 5 Team Scores				
Step 6 Average of Individual Scores				
Step 7 Gain Scores				
Step 8 The Lowest Score in the Team				
Step 9 The Number of Individual Scores Lower than the Team Score				

Exercise F. The following exercise on the *project cycle* is given to the group which applies the same process as in *Exercise E*.

The Project Cycle Exercise[3]

The Situation

You are a team of international consultants specialized in the design and management of development projects.

The government of a developing country has asked you to provide advise on how to organize development projects in the most effective way.

The Task

On the next page is a list of twenty activities (A through T) all related to the so-called *Project Cycle*. These activities are presented at random. Your task is to rank them according to the logical sequence typical of a sound project cycle.

Step 1: Without talking to anyone, rank order the 20 activities presented in Figure 29 starting with "1" as being the first activity typical of the project cycle and "20" the last one.

Step 2. As a team, agree on a common ranking for the same twenty activities.

---

[3]Developed by P. Casse in cooperation with a group of participants in a seminar for Development Bankers organized by the Economic Development Institute of the World Bank and the Association of Development Financing Institutions for Asia and the Pacific, Washington, DC, January 12-16, 1981.

Figure 29. Project Cycle Activities

PROJECT CYCLE ACTIVITIES	STEP 1 Individual Ranking	STEP 2 Team Ranking	STEP 3 Experts' Ranking	STEP 4 Difference between Step 1 and 3	STEP 5 Difference between Step 2 and 3
A. Select project					
B. Determine alternative ways to accomplish the project objectives					
C. Gather information about the National Development Plan					
D. Agree upon a loan document					
E. Set up the objectives of the project					
F. Measure the importance of various projects in relation to the plan and the sector concerned					
G. Appraise the soundness of the project in technical, economic, commercial, financial, managerial and organizational terms					
H. Finalize preliminary feasibility studies and reports					
I. Write a project completion report					

J. Prioritize projects according to importance and feasibility						
K. Assess the relative importance (in economic and social terms) of the sectors covered in the National Plan						
L. Negotiate the lending conditions						
M. Monitor the project progress						
N. Identify the position of the government regarding the various sectors and projects						
O. Adapt the project to changing circumstances						
P. Study the feasibility of several key projects which have the support of the government						
Q. Implement the project according to schedule						
R. Manage procurement process according to international competitive bidding rules						
S. Collect data on the technical economic, commercial, financial, managerial and organizational dimensions of the project						
T. Award contracts						

TOTALS:

The Experts' Ranking[4]

Phase 1 Identification	C	1
	K	2
	F	3
	N	4
	P	5
	J	6
	A	7
Phase 2 Preparations	E	8
	S	9
	B	10
	H	11
Phase 3 Approaches	G	12
Phase 4 Negotiation	L	13
	D	14
Phase 5 Implementation	R	15
	T	16
	Q	17
Phase 6 Supervision	M	18
	O	19
	I	20

---

[4]W.C. Baum, "The World Bank Project Cycle," *Finance and Development,* December 1978.

Issues and Questions for the group:

• Find at least three cultural definitions of a *project*.

• Identify some of the basic assumptions which are behind the use of a "National Development Plan."

• What does the item "Prioritize projects according to importance and feasibility" tell you from a cross-cultural perspective?

Exercise G. The eight trigrams representative of the flow of energy forces operating in individuals and groups as described in the I CHING or book of changes[5] are introduced to the group.

Figure 30. I Ching Trigrams

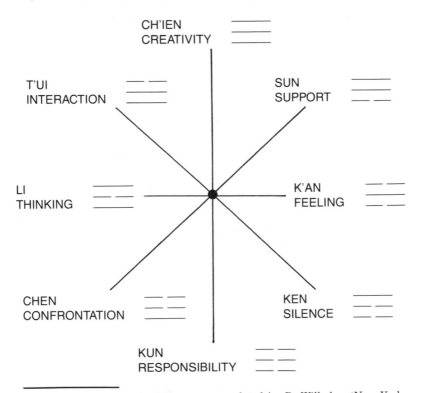

---

[5]The I CHING or Book of Changes, translated by R. Wilhelm, (New York: Princeton University Press, 1977). The text is reprinted from: J.W. Pfeiffer and J.E. Jones (Eds.), *The 1976 Annual Handbook for Group Facilitators*. San Diego, CA: University Associates, 1976. Used with permission.

1. Ch'ien (══════), the creative, heaven. Associated with energy, strength, and excitement, it represents the pole of *creative power.*

2. K'un (══ ══), the receptive, earth, is associated with the womb, nourishment, the great wagon of the earth that carries all life. It represents the pole of *yielding, docile responsivity.*

3. Chen (══ ══), the arousing, thunder. It is associated with movement, speed, expansion, and anger. In terms of human polarities, the sign represents *confrontation.*

4. Sun (══════), the gentle, penetrating wind. Associated with gentle persuasion, quiet decision-making, and problem-solving, this sign represents the pole of *support.*

5. K'an (══ ══), the abysmal, water. It is associated with toil, hard work, danger, perseverance, and melancholy. It represents *the pole of body and feeling.*

6. Li (══ ══), the clinging, fire. It is associated with dependency, but also with conceptual clarity and perception. It represents the pole of *intellect and mind.*

7. Ken (══ ══), keeping still, the mountain. Associated with fidelity, meditation, and watchfulness, it represents the pole of *reflective silence.*

8. T'ui (══ ══), the joyous, lake. This sign is associated with the pleasures of the mouth: eating, talking, singing. It represents the pole of *joyful interaction.*

The group is asked to use the model and analyze:

(1) The various phases a team goes through when working on an issue

(2) What happens when two opposite poles meet, i.e. intellect + feeling

(3) What occurs when a team is stuck at one pole

(4) The impact of the integration of more than two poles, i.e. support + confrontation + silence + creativity

(5) Individuals' relations to the polarities

Exercise H. The ten questions below are designed to assess the participants' sensitivity toward intercultural team building.

Instructions

Check each item and tabulate the results before looking at the next page:

Intercultural Team Building (ITB)	Strongly Disagree 1	Disagree 2	Undecided 3	Agree 4	Strongly Agree 5
1. Disagreements and conflicts are usual and expected in ITB.					
2. Most people are reserved when they join an intercultural team.					
3. Consensus is quite critical in an intercultural team.					
4. Intercultural teams take more time to build upon their resources.					
5. Anxiety should be dealt with in an intercultural team.					
6. Rotating leadership helps ITB.					
7. Many individuals have an identity problem when working in an intercultural team.					
8. Power is a critical issue in ITB.					
9. Each team should be responsible for maintaining and improving relations in an intercultural team.					
10. Intercultural teams can be (if properly managed) more creative than other teams.					

A score between 40 and 50 reveals a very good sensitivity to Intercultural Team Building; between 20 and 40 a fair one; between 10 and 20 a poor one.

Exercise I. The following statements are checked by the group:

(1)

Japanese Team Building	True	False
1. Japanese are concerned with losing face.		
2. Japanese value self-control.		
3. Japanese reward individual achievements.		
4. Seniority is important and highly respected.		
5. Japanese value decisions made by consensus.		

(2)

Latin American Team Building	True	False
1. Training is highly valued by Latin Americans.		
2. Personal pride is critical in team building.		
3. Latin Americans have an inclination for action, competitiveness.		
4. Latin Americans can be formal at times.		
5. Strong leadership is looked for.		

(3)

African Team Building	True	False
1. The tribe still provides the guidelines for accepted behavior in many African groups.		
2. Africans are fatalist.		
3. Trust and confidence are highly valued.		
4. Africans strongly believe in friendship which comes before task achievement.		
5. Group participation is encouraged.		

(4)

French Team Building	True	False
1. French believe in enjoying life.		
2. Imaginative, they like to play with ideas.		
3. French are status-conscious.		
4. French like to be liked.		
5. Disagreements are perceived as good and stimulating.		

(5)

Middle East Team Building	True	False
1. Religion has an impact on almost everything in Arabic cultures.		
2. Arabs value eloquence.		
3. Compliments and well presented flattery are appreciated.		
4. Arabs do not like hard bargains.		
5. Expressive and sensitive people are liked.		

Exercise J. Six volunteers sit around a table in the middle of the room. A seventh participant is selected as the leader of the "intercultural team."

The Task

"Your team has 30 minutes to come up with as many criteria as possible for assessing the effectiveness of the intercultural team. In other words, your task is to answer the following question: How do we know that an intercultural team is effective?"

Instruction for the team leader

"You must lead the discussion so that the team will accomplish its objective as efficiently as possible. You must know that your task is not going to be easy since the team members belong to different cultures. It is up to you to (a) identify the main characteristics of their behavior and (b) act accordingly."

Instructions for the team members (one per member)

"This is confidential. Do not share your instructions with anybody. Try to stick to your guidelines as closely as possible during the entire exercise."

Team Member 1: You belong to a culture in which challenging the leader of a team is valued. Try to take the leadership of the team.

Team Member 2: To be passive is highly respected in your culture. It is a sign of wisdom and self-control. Do not show any interest in the team.

Team Member 3: You strongly believe in achieving. Do your best so that the team objective will be reached.

Team Member 4: Support your leader and be cooperative. Your culture highly values (a) respect for the leader and (b) teamwork. Ease the communication and interaction processes in the team.

Team Member 5: Your culture is strongly "idea-oriented." The subject given to the team does not appeal to you. Try to push the team in another direction and discuss something else.

Team Member 6: You believe in competition as well as in conflicts. Be aggressive towards the other members of the team. Push them around.

The group dynamics as well as the criteria (see Input 2-B) are discussed when the exercise is over.

Exercise K. Three *creativity methods* are experienced by the participants:

1. The Scenario Technique

a. Overall description. This approach consists of assuming that a problem has been solved in an ideal fashion. It focuses on a description of the ideal situation which would exist if the best decision were made.

b. Method. The exercise is organized as follows.

Phase 1: The group clarifies the decision to be made or problem to be solved (10 minutes).

Phase 2: It starts to describe the ideal situation with all its advantages assuming that the right decision was made (25 minutes).

Phase 3: The group goes back to the problem at hand and formulates a decision using what has been learned through the process (15 minutes).

c. Illustration. A group of managers who had to make a proposal regarding a new performance appraisal system for their own organization spent the first few minutes visualizing an ideal situation using their imagination as much as possible before tackling the given task.

d. Exercises

- A company is concerned with the preparation of its employees for overseas assignments. Assuming that you are a team of intercultural consultants, what kind of intercultural orientation program (content and process) would you recommend?

- It has been shown that "culture-specific" approaches for briefing people for overseas work can be misleading and dangerous. What do you suggest?

- You have been assigned to manage an intercultural team for the first time. How are you going to approach this task in order to be effective?

2. The Synectic Technique

a. Overall description. This approach consists of moving away from the topic to be analyzed or the decision to be made and focusing for a while on something completely different in order to come up with completely new and fresh ideas and seeing the problem from a completely different angle.

b. Method. The exercise is organized as follows.

Phase 1: The group clarifies the decision to be made or the problem to be solved (10 minutes).

Phase 2: It selects a topic to be discussed. It has to be as far away as possible from the assigned or chosen pattern (5 minutes).

Phase 3: The group discusses the selected topic (20 minutes).

Phase 4: The discussion stops and goes back to the real problem at hand. The group uses as many free associations as possible between the given problem and the discussed topic (15 minutes).

c. Illustration. A group of managers that was supposed to discuss a reorganization first spent some time analyzing the *blood circulation system* before tackling the given task using some of the ideas they had imitated and extrapolated from them.

d. Exercises

- You are the leader of an intercultural team and one of the team members is overcritical and disrupts the harmony (and effectiveness) of the teamwork. What do you do?

• Set up a performance appraisal system for intercultural teams.

• How would you reinforce the achievement motivation for a team which is basically affiliation-oriented?

3. The Delphi Technique

a. Overall description. This approach consists of organizing a series of brainstorming sessions with various small groups which work at the same time on identical issues without being in touch with one another in order to restrict psychological interference and reinforce the creativity of the group members.

b. Method. The process goes like this.

Phase 1: A central unit is set up in addition to two or three small groups which meet either in different rooms or in the same room but without seeing one another.

Phase 2: The central unit poses the same first question to the groups and registers their answers (there is no need for the groups to know what the problem is!).

Phase 3: The various responses and reactions are given to the groups, which comment on them.

Phase 4: The process goes on until the time when the central unit is pleased with the results of the "blind interactions."

c. Illustration. A group had to define the concept of time in a completely new way. The central unit organized its questions around a set of themes such as biology, road circulation, life, death, etc. The result was astonishing.

d. Exercises

• Define the concept of multicultural management.

• What are the main qualifications required from a multicultural manager?

• How to convince the president of a multinational that his organization needs intercultural training programs for its managers?

Exercise L. The following case study is presented and discussed:

Teamwork and The Art of Listening[6]

The chief executive of an international organization and his top management group (about 15 people) have asked a good mid-level

---

[6]Created by Mr. R.H. Springuel of the Economic Development Institute of the World Bank.

manager to temporarily leave his managerial position and advise on how to improve the internal functioning of the bank. After four months the adviser sends a confidential report, recommending to the chief executive a six-month program to experiment with a more participatory management style, i.e. for the managers concerned to change their behavior. A meeting is called, and, the night before the meeting, three members of the management group warn the adviser that they will say plainly that he has written nonsense.

The next day, understandably apprehensive, the adviser presents briefly his proposal. The chief executive looks smilingly around the table and the silence seems eternal. He widens his smile and asks whether the silence means that all agree with the adviser...and the silence is more impressive than ever. With an even bigger smile he says that he likes the adviser's proposals. Before he has finished his statement, eight hands are raising including those of the three critics of the report. All have very positive comments and suggestions and constructive questions, and the adviser's recommendations are discussed and adopted without a single dissent. The adviser is asked to implement his proposals and to report to the same top group at the end of the six month experimental program, with recommendation for a further and presumably larger program.

Minutes of this meeting and recommendations are distributed to the whole staff. Subsequently, the adviser is prevented from implementing *any* part of his program by middle level managers, and his short report at the end of the six months never reaches the chief executive, who in turn, never asks for another meeting on the subject.

Question: In the top management meeting why wouldn't anyone say anything before the chief executive had spoken? Why were the proposals approved by all members of the meeting including the three who disagreed with the proposals? Why did the adviser, who knew of this opposition, remain silent? Why didn't the chief executive ever ask for the report on the experimental program? Did the chief executive really listen to the adviser when approving his proposals? Who could have done what, differently?

5. Time: Between one and two days.

6. Conceptual Framework:

INPUT 1

Figure 31. Intercultural Team Building: A Model

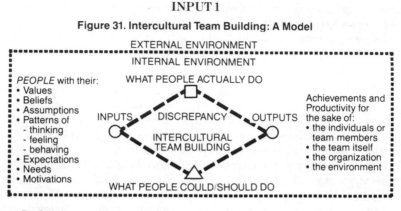

Definitions

(a) **Intercultural teamwork** is the process by which a group of individuals from different cultures try systematically to use a set of internal and external resources in order to achieve some objectives (selected by the team, imposed upon them, or a mixture of both) in the best possible way (at a minimum economic, psychological, social, and cultural cost).

(b) **Intercultural team building** is the process by which the gap between what people from various cultures actually do and what they should or could do for the sake of the team members, the team itself, the organization, and its environment.

INPUT 2

A

Synergy as defined by A.G. Banet can be obtained through the use of three basic teamwork skills, namely:

1. Active listening

• Everybody in the team has a chance to speak up and all ideas are listened to.

• Everybody does not talk at the same time; team members do not interrupt one another; they do not jump from one subject to another.

• People practice empathy and try to see what other members of the team see.

2. Supporting

- Team members focus upon what's right in an idea expressed by someone instead of shooting at it ("I can see three good things in your idea…").

- People feel they can take a risk and freely express themselves. A maximum of ideas is recorded.

- Participants build upon one another's ideas. They do not use the "yes…but…" expression. They say: "yes…and…"

3. Differing

- The "expert syndrome" is avoided and all ideas are probed and questioned.

- Group thinks and oversupport are avoided.

- Conflicts and disagreements are accepted (at least at this stage in the process).

B

Criteria for recognizing an effective intercultural team:

(1) Interdependence is valued by the team members.

(2) Confrontations and conflicts lead to (a) a probing of assumptions that people have; and (b) an improvement in creativity (more and better ideas are produced).

(3) Objectives are understood by the members of the team who share a minimum of common values, beliefs, and assumptions.

(4) The team is able to review its ongoing dynamic from time to time.

(5) The team is open to the external "world" (good connections with other teams, organizations, etc.).

(6) Humor is frequently expressed within the team.

(7) The team is perceived by its members as a "learning community."

(8) The team activities appeal to the members' imagination, intellect, senses, and emotions.

(9) The team grows with its operations.

(10) The team is able to create its own value system to fit the situation it has to cope with.

7. Handouts and Readings:

(a) Handouts

Adler, N., "Designing a Culturally Synergistic Organization," *The Bridge*, Fall 1981.

Banet, A.G., "Yin/Yang: A Perspective on Theories of Group Development," *The 1976 Annual Handbook for Group Facilitators*, pp. 169-184.

Chambers, P., "Matching Personalities to Create Effective Teams," *International Management*, 28:20-4, November 1973.

Chopra, A., "Motivation in Task-Oriented Groups," *Journal of Nursing Administration*, January-February 1973.

Condon, J., "Narvhodo! How very Japanese!," *The Bridge*, Summer 1981.

Condon, J., "...So Near the United States," *The Bridge*, Spring 1980.

Davis, S.M., "U.S. versus Latin America: Business and Culture," *Harvard Business Review*, November-December 1969.

Distefano, J.J., "Managing in Other Cultures: Some Do's and Some Don'ts," *The Business Quarterly*, Autumn 1972, pp. 22-23.

Drucker, P.A., "What We Can Learn from Japanese Management," *The McKinsey Quarterly*, Winter 1973.

Drucker, P.F., "New Templates for Today's Organizations," *Harvard Business Review*, January-February 1974.

Ely, D.D., "Team Building for Creativity," *Personnel Journal*, 54: 226-7, April 1975.

Gardner, N.D., "The Spiral Analysis Method as a Training Aid in Learning to Listen," *The Journal of the American Society of Training Directors*, November-December 1956.

Harris, P.R., "Cultural Awareness Training for Human Resource Development," *Training and Development Journal*, March 1979.

Harris, P.R., "Managing Cultural Differences," *The Bridge*, Spring 1979.

Harris, P.R., "Professional Synergy," *Training and Development Journal*, January 1981.

Harris, P.R., "Synergy in Organizational Culture," *The Bridge*, Fall 1981.

Horovitz, J.H., "Management Control in France, Great Britain and Germany," *Columbia Journal of World Business,* Summer 1978, pp. 16-22.

Johnson, A.J., and Ouchi, W.G., "Made in America (Under Japanese Management)," *Harvard Business Review,* September-October 1974.

Katz, R.L., "Human Relations Skills Can Be Sharpened," *Harvard Business Review,* Vol. 34, 1956, pp. 61-72.

Levy, D., "The Story of Z," *Passages,* September 1981.

McGregor, D., "Teamwork and Tensions," *The Professional Manager,* Chapter 10, 1967, pp. 160-181.

Nath, R., "Training International Business and Management Personnel: A Contingency Approach," *Overview of Intercultural Education, Training and Research, Vol. II: Education and Training,* SIETAR, May 1978.

Nowotny, O.H., "American versus European Management Philosophy," *Harvard Business Review,* March-April 1964.

Ouchi, W.G., and Jaeger, A.M., "Type Z Corporation: Stability in the Midst of Mobility," *Academy of Management Review,* April 1978.

Palleschi, P., and Heim, P., "The Hidden Barriers to Team Building," *Training and Development Journal,* July 1980.

Reddin, W.J., "Making the Team Work," *Business Management,* 99:26-8, February 1969.

Sherwood, J.J., and Hoylman, F.M., "Utilizing Human Resources: Individual versus Group Approaches to Problem Solving and Decision-Making," *The 1978 Annual Handbook for Group Facilitators,* pp. 157-162.

Slomon, L.N., "Team Development: A Training Approach," *The 1977 Annual Handbook for Group Facilitators,* pp. 181-193.

Vaill, P.B., "Towards a Behavioral Description of High-Performing Systems," *OD Practitioner,* Vol. 9, No. 2, May 1977.

Vicker, R., "Understanding the Oral Psyche," *Wall Street Journal,* October 19, 1973.

Wilemon, D.L., and Thamhain, H.J., "Team Building in Project Management," Paper presented at the Project Management Institute's Eleventh Annual Seminar Symposium, Atlanta, Georgia, October 1979.

Zemke, R., "Team Building: Helping People Learn to Work Together", and "Committees: Will Forming One Really Help?" *Training HRD*, February 1978, pp. 23-26.

(b) Readings

Barzini, L., *The Italians*. New York: Bantam Books, 1969.

Chomsky, N., *Problems of Knowledge and Freedom*. New York: Vintage Books, 1971.

Davis, S.M., *Comparative Management: Organizational and Cultural Perspectives*. Englewood Cliffs, NJ: Prentice-Hall, 1971.

Downs, J.F., *Cultures in Crisis*. Beverly Hills, California: Glencoe Press, 1975.

Dyer, W.L., *Team Building: Issues and Alternatives*. Reading, Mass: Addison-Wesley, 1977.

Feig, J.P., and Blair, J.G., *There is a Difference: Twelve Intercultural Perspectives*. Washington, DC: Meridian House International, 1975.

Greenberg, S., *Management: American and European Styles*. Belmont, California: Wadsworth Publishing Company, Inc., 1970.

Hall, S., and Lindzey, G., *Theories of Personality*. New York: Wiley, 1957.

Heenan, D.A., and Perlmutter, H.V., *Multinational Organization Development*. Reading, Mass: Addison-Wesley, 1979.

Johnson, D.W., and Johnson, F.P., *Joining Together (Group Theory and Group Skills)*. Englewood Cliffs, NJ: Prentice-Hall, Inc., 1975.

Lasch, C., *The Culture of Narcissism*. New York: W.W. Norton & Company, Inc., 1978.

Leary, T., *Interpersonal Diagnosis of Personality*. New York: Ronald, 1957.

Leavitt, H.J., *Managerial Psychology*. Chicago: University of Chicago, 1964.

Liebmang, S.B., *Exploring the Latin American Mind*. Chicago: Nelson-Hall, 1976.

Luft, J., *Group Process (An Introduction to Group Dynamics)*. Palo Alto, California: National Press Books, 1963.

Maccoby, M., *The Leader: Managing the Work Place*. New York: Simon & Schuster, 1981.

Merry, U., and Allerhand, M.E., *Developing Teams and Organizations.* Reading, Mass: Addison-Wesley, 1977.

Minami, H., *Psychology of the Japanese People.* Ontario: University Press, 1972.

Mitchell, T.R., *People in Organizations: Understanding Their Behavior.* New York: McGraw-Hill, 1978.

Moran, R.T., and Harris, P.R., *Managing Cultural Synergy.* Houston: Gulf Publishing Co., 1982.

Munroe, R. and R., *Cross-Cultural Human Development.* Monterey, California: Brooks/Cole, 1975.

Osborn, A.F., *Applied Imagination.* New York: Scribner, 1957.

Ouchi, W., *Theory Z (How American Business Can Meet the Japanese Challenge).* Reading, Mass: Addison-Wesley, 1981.

Patton, B.R., and Giffin, K., *Problem-Solving Group Interaction.* New York: Harper and Row, 1973.

Prince, G.M., *The Practice of Creativity.* New York: Harper and Row, 1970.

Prosser, M.H., *The Cultural Dialogue.* Boston, Mass: Houghton Mifflin Co., 1978.

Rudhyar, D., *Culture, Crisis and Creativity.* Rochelle Park, NJ: Hayden Book Company, Inc., 1978.

Schultz, W., *Firo, A Three-Dimensional Theory of Interpersonal Behavior.* New York: Holt, Rinehart and Winston, 1958.

Smith, M., *The Russians.* New York: Ballantine, 1976.

Turnbell, C., *Man in Africa.* New York: Anchor Press, 1977.

Zalensnik, A., and Moment, D., *The Dynamics of Interpersonal Behavior.* New York: Wiley, 1964.

"C'est à l'encadrement de se mettre au service des hommes et non aux hommes de se mettre au service de l'encadrement."

R. Colin

"It is up to the structures to be adjusted to people and not to people to be adjusted to structures." P. Casse (free translation)

Workshop 5
Participative Management: Who wants to participate?

---

1. Introduction: A great confusion exists among managers and employees regarding the meaning and the concrete implications of participation. Furthermore, people with different cultural backgrounds will define and understand participative management according to their *dominant value orientations*. Some people will insist on the involvement in the objective-setting process. Others will stress the importance of active participation in the selection and implementation of the appropriate strategies and tactics in order to achieve the objectives. A third group of people will insist on the outcome of the participative process, namely, the fair distribution of the products of all investments (economic and social) made by the people concerned within an organization or a project.

It seems to me that the main idea or value which underlies participative management is to make sure that all the members of an organizational culture are - and remain - active in and committed to the development of their working environment, not only for the sake of productivity and profits, but also for the purpose of enhancing their own professional and personal growth. Participative management is not a panacea. It can be counterproductive and dangerous. Well applied, it leads to the creation of a *humanistic organization*. Ill applied, it is pure manipulation and creates frustration as well as cynicism.

2. Aim: To analyze and understand *participative management* from a cross-cultural viewpoint.

3. Objectives:

(a) define participative management (group discussion);

(b) identify various types of participation (group discussion and conceptual framework: Input 1);

(c) assess the manager's and employee's attitudes regarding participative management according to four value orientations (group discussion);

(d) analyze the input of a set of cultural assumptions on the practice of participative management (exercise);

(e) relate the participative development process to management, and more specifically, to the management of a development project in an African culture (case study and conceptual framework: Input 2).

4. Process:

Exercise A. Participants meet in trios and each individual writes down his or her own definition (one sentence) on a small card: "Participative management is...." When ready, they exchange their cards (one each) and interpret what another member of the group means. The member who has written the sentence listens to the interpreter without making any comments. When the process is finished (the three interpretations have been made), then team members share their impressions regarding the meanings given to their own definitions.

Exercise B. Participants are split into sub-groups of four to six and work on the following assignments:

• Assuming that you are a team of specialists in management, prepare a statement about the various types of participation that organizations should be concerned with.

• Identify 10 expectations that managers have when they envision participative management.

• Identify 10 expectations that employees have when they try to promote participative management.

Exercise C. The trainer presents the theory on the four value orientations and their impact on communication:[1]

Four value orientations can be found in any individual and anywhere in the world. They are the *action, process, people,* and *idea* orientations. Everybody has a value orientation which is more important than the others. It is called the *dominant value orientation.* The main characteristics of the four value orientations in terms of their impact on people's lifestyles can be described as follows:

• *Action-oriented* people like action, doing, achieving, getting things done, improving, moving ahead, being pragmatic (down to earth), being direct or to the point, decisive, and challenging.

• *Process-oriented* people like facts, organizing, structuring, setting up strategies, tactics, analyzing, documenting, testing, controlling, observing, being systematic, logical, unemotional, cautious, and patient.

---

[1]Casse, *Training for the Cross-Cultural Mind*, pp. 125-132.

• *People-oriented* individuals like to focus on social processes, interactions, motivation, teamwork, communication, feelings, needs, expectations, personal growth, and self-actualization. They are spontaneous, emphatic, warm, perceptive, sensitive, emotional, and subjective.

• *Idea-oriented* people like concepts, theories, innovation, creativity, opportunities, possibilities, and new ways and approaches to problem-solving. They are imaginative, charismatic, full of ideas, provocative and stimulating.

The group is then asked to work on a problem while four observers try to identify each individual's dominant value orientation using the four checklists provided hereunder.

Step 1: *The Problem* (see Figure 32)

"Using the small train which is in the station and following the track, groups must switch the positions of wagons A and B which cannot go through the tunnel that is too narrow (only the locomotive can do so). The train has to be put back in the station by the end of the exercise." (See solution under Input 1-A.)

Figure 32. The Small Train Exercise

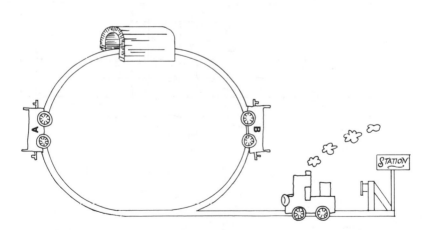

Step 2: The following four checklists[2] are given to the observers. Each of them concentrates either on one dominant value orientation and all team members, or on one team member (in the case of a team of four) and all four value orientations.

SURVEY OF VALUE ORIENTATIONS

(CHECKLISTS)

Instructions for the Observers

Check each statement which describes the value orientation(s) of the listed team member(s).

Identification of Value Orientation #1	Team Members										
Dominant Value Orientation #1											
1. In my view, this member is *ACTION*-oriented, to the extent that he/she:											
— considers deadlines important											
— wants to set his/her own objectives											
— becomes impatient with long deliberations											
— likes to handle several projects at the same time											
— searches for challenging tasks											
— likes to achieve											
— is impatient with long, slow assignments											
— likes to get things done											
— usually jumps from one task to another											
— likes brief, to-the-point statements											
ACTION Total											

[2]The four checklists have been developed and used by the World Health Organization in some of its training programs. For more information contact Dr. W. Barton, WHO, Geneva, Switzerland.

Identification of Value Orientation #2   **Team Members**

Dominant Value Orientation #2											
2. In my view, this member is *PROCESS*-oriented, to the extent that he/she:											
— deals with problems in a systematic way											
— likes new ideas to be tested before they are used											
— considers the step-by-step approach effective											
— is cool under pressure											
— maintains that analysis should always precede action											
— relies on observation and data											
— wants key decisions made in a cautious way											
— thinks that emotions create problems											
— likes to organize											
— is patient with details											
PROCESS Total											

Identification of Value Orientation #3   **Team Members**

Dominant Value Orientation #3											
3. In my view, this member is *PEOPLE*-oriented, to the extent that he/she:											
— enjoys working with people											
— basically tries to understand other people's emotions											
— is sensitive to others' needs											
— considers cooperation a key word											
— is able to assess the climate of a group											
— can express his/her feelings openly											
— likes to be liked by others											
— considers good relationships to be essential											
— learns by interacting with others											
— is confident in himself/herself											
PEOPLE Total											

Identification of Value Orientation #4   **Team Members**

Dominant Value Orientation #4											
4. In my view, this member is *IDEA*-oriented, to the extent that he/she:											
— enjoys innovation very much											
— is more interested in the future than the past											
— challenges people around him/her											
— likes creative problem-solving											
— is a fast thinker											
— does not like details											
— has a tendency to start things and not finish them											
— likes designing new projects											
— tries out his/her ideas on people											
— enjoys playing with ideas											
IDEA Total											

Final Tabulation

Instructions: Determine for each team member the value orientation that has the highest number of checks and insert "1" for that orientation, "2" for the second highest, and so on (in the case of identical totals, give the same rank number and move down e.g. 1,2,3,4).

                                                              Team Members

Four Value Orientations - Ranking											
ACTION											
PROCESS											
PEOPLE											
IDEA											

Step 3: Instructions for Each Team

Taking your dominant value orientation into account identify at least 10 characteristics of the way you look at participative management assuming that (a) you are a manager and (b) you are an employee (five for each).

Subjects / Value Orientations	Managers	Employees
Action Orientations	1. 2. 3. 4. 5.	1. 2. 3. 4. 5.
Process Orientations	1. 2. 3. 4. 5.	1. 2. 3. 4. 5.
People Orientations	1. 2. 3. 4. 5.	1. 2. 3. 4. 5.
Idea Orientations	1. 2. 3. 4. 5.	1. 2. 3. 4. 5.

Step 4: The four sub-groups or teams share their characteristics and compare them with the list below (Figure 33), to be distributed after the participants have had a chance to discuss their findings.

Figure 33. Four Value Orientations and their Impact on Managers and Employees

Subjects / Value Orientations	Managers	Employees
Action Orientations	1. Make decisions and discuss them with employees. 2. Like quick decisions. 3. Like to set up objectives and delegate execution. 4. Monitor action on an ad hoc basis. 5. Can be impatient with employees.	1. Want to set up their own objectives. 2. Like to work on their own projects. 3. Are sensitive to feedback. 4. Act sometimes without thinking. 5. Are interested in professional and personal growth.
Process Orientations	1. Spend time clarifying objectives with employees. 2. Collect facts before making decisions. 3. Give special importance to strategies and tactics. 4. Monitor actions in a systematic way (use of check points). 5. Like to think things through.	1. Do not like to be pushed around. 2. Like to propose options, analyze alternatives. 3. Want to know how their work fits into the overall operation. 4. Seek orders. 5. Are patient with details.
People Orientations	1. Believe that people are full of resources. 2. Search for consensus. 3. Encourage teamwork. 4. Provide recognition easily. 5. Delegate responsibility for control and monitoring.	1. Enjoy meetings. 2. Like to feel that they belong to a team. 3. Need to know they are supported by the manager. 4. Sometimes lose sight of the task at hand. 5. Are oversensitive to others reactions.
Idea Orientations	1. Like stimulating exchanges with employees. 2. Have a tendancy to start too many projects at the same time. 3. Make long-term decisions. 4. Delegate in an informal way. 5. Are bored with routine activities.	1. Want to be involved in special projects. 2. Look for innovative actions. 3. Enjoy brainstorming sessions. 4. Assess their managers on the originality of their ideas. 5. Are bold and are sometimes misunderstood by their managers.

After having had an opportunity to compare their own lists with the above matrix, the groups discuss the interactions between people with different profiles, i.e. an action-oriented manager who works with a process-oriented employee. They can also explore the relations between an idea-oriented manager and a team made up of people who are basically action-oriented. The group can decide on what they want to analyze.

Step 5: When they have finished they then apply what they have learned to the following case study.

CASE STUDY

You are a group of consultants and have been invited to advise an employee of an organization (multinational) on a problem that she has. Here is what she says to you:

> "I feel myself to be more competent and more dynamic than my boss who is a quiet, reserved, and rather political manager. My own style of open confrontation on issues works well for me but it has led my supervisor to downgrade me on appraisals of my work relationships. I have let him know that I disagree with his evaluation in this area, and that I feel that the style which he views as a handicap is actually one of my best assets. I am now getting the feeling that I'm hurting my career by being faced with this confrontation. What can I do?"

Questions:

1. Identify the various value orientations that characterize the two people involved.

2. Assess the impact of those value orientations on the relations between the two characters as well as on their definitions of participative management.

3. Prepare a set of concrete recommendations (a) for the manager; and (b) for the employee.

4. Analyze your recommendations taking your own dominant value orientation into account.

5. Find at least one other illustration of the kind of confrontations people experience because of their differences of value orientations.

Exercise D. The group is asked to study the following three "critical incidents" and identify as many cultural values, beliefs, and assumptions as possible behind what the individuals say or do.

Critical Incident #1

Manager - I have received your leave slip and I must tell you that I do not like the way you did it!

Employee - What do you mean?

Manager - You know very well what I mean....

Employee - No, I do not. What have I done wrong this time?

Manager - You do know that you should have discussed your plan with me before finalizing it. A minimum of cooperation is needed. We'll have chaos in this unit if we do not organize ourselves together.

Employee - But I am here to discuss it.

Manager - Now it's too late!

Critical Incident #2

Manager - John, as you know it is time for your anniversary evaluation or performance appraisal (I do not like to call it that). I think it is a good opportunity for you and me to sit back and take stock of what has happened in the last twelve months, assess your strengths, and build upon them.

Employee - Fair enough.

Manager - Good! So what I would like to do is to ask you to evaluate your own performance first (some kind of self-evaluation if you do not mind), put it in a draft and then we shall discuss it.

Employee - Well...I do not know...

Manager - What do you mean?

Employee - Well....I don't like to much....

Manager - I do not understand. Are you telling me that you do not want to assess your own strengths and weaknesses?

Employee - ....

Manager - Come on, John. Speak up.

Employee - Well...yes, I do mind. I do not think that I should go first. I know what my performance was, its positive and negative aspects. Now, I want you to tell me what you think of it. It is unfair to reverse the process and I prefer not to do it.

Manager - ....

Critical Incident #3

The following dialogue takes place between a manager and his employees (20 people):

Manager - I understand that there is a "morale problem" in our unit....what is it?

Employees - .... (silence)

Manager - Come on! You are the ones who preach participation all the time. Here you are. Speak out!

Employees .... (silence - some people smile, others look at the ceiling, others are obviously embarrassed)

Manager - How do you want me to do something about the problem if you don't explain to me what it is all about....?

Employees - .... (silence)

Manager - Alright. I'll see what I can do. Next on the agenda.....

Exercise E. Hereunder is a list of 20 stereotypical value orientations related to some Latin American cultures.[3] Participants analyze their impact on the practice of participative management:

1. A greater importance is given to abstracts (or abstract ideas) than to facts (or factual arrangements).

2. Latin Americans have a tendency to switch from apathy to frantic activity (they have many "ups and downs").

3. They are highly sensual and more interested in the arts, poetry, beauty, and esthetics than in practicality.

4. Inner dignity and worth of the individual is highly valued ("Dignidad de la persona").

5. "Compadres" in work relationships call for a working-socializing climate.

6. Delegation of responsibility and authority is avoided because of fear of competition and loss of control.

7. "Machismo" or protection of manhood is important. Women have to be protected; their basic role is being a wife, mother, and companion.

---

[3]P.R. Harris, and R.T. Moran, "Case Study: Que Pasa? The Latin American Influence," *Managing Cultural Differences* (Houston: Gulf Publishing Co., 1979), pp. 257-269.

8. Regard for social status and prestige are more desirable than money.

9. Knowledge or reality is derived from intuitive sources rather than objective experience and reflection.

10. Great importance is given to one's immediate and extended family as a source of identity and security.

11. Social distinctions are based on family connection and land-holdings.

12. Men are stratified in a social hierarchy where they find security and dignity.

13. Change is not highly valued.

14. "Personalismo" is very important. Trust is placed only in those with whom one shares a personal relationship.

15. Latin Americans have difficulty in organizing themselves. Very often they are either under- or over-organized.

16. The professions are more highly valued than business enterprise. Humanism is more valued than pragmatic action.

17. Business opportunities are guided by social and political influence.

18. Spiritual and humanistic, rather than commercial, values are admired. Religion is personalistic, characterized by "spiritualism" and "superstition."

19. Downward control of information is practiced.

20. Timelessness and fate are related; one flows into the other (the concept of mañana).

Exercise F. The following comparative study (Figure 34) between Japanese, North American and Latin American negotiation styles can also be used in order to identify various interpretations of participative management.

Figure 34. Negotiation Styles From A Cross-Cultural Perspective[4]

JAPANESE	NORTH AMERICAN	LATIN AMERICAN
Emotional sensitivity highly valued.	Emotional sensitivity not highly valued.	Emotional sensitivity valued.
Hiding of emotions.	Dealing straightforwardly/ impersonally.	Emotional/Passionate
Subtle power plays; conciliation.	Litigation not as much as conciliation.	Great power plays; exploitation of weak.
Loyalty to employer. Employer takes care of its employees.	Lack of commitment to employer. Breaking of ties by either if necessary.	Loyalty to employer (who is often family).
Group decision-making consensus.	Teamwork provides input to a decision-maker.	Decisions come down from one individual.
Face-saving crucial. Decisions often made on basis of saving someone from embarrassment.	Decisions made on a cost/ benefit basis. Face-saving does not always matter.	Face-saving crucial in decision-making to preserve honor, dignity.
Decision-makers openly influenced by special interests.	Decision-makers influenced by special interests but often not considered ethical.	Execution of special interests of decision-maker expected, condoned.
Not argumentative. Quiet when right.	Argumentative when right or wrong, but impersonal.	Argumentative when right or wrong; passionate.
What is down in writing must be accurate, valid.	Great importance given to documentation as evidential proof.	Impatient with documentation as obstacle to understanding general principles.
Step-by-step approach to decision-making.	Methodically organized decision-making.	Impulsive, erratic decision-making.
Good of group is the ultimate aim.	Profit motive or good of individual ultimate aim.	What is good for group is good for the individual.
Cultivate a good emotional/ social setting for decision-making. Get to know decision-makers.	Decision-making impersonal. Avoid involvements, conflict of interest.	Personalism necessary for good decision-making.

Exercise G. Presentation of a case study related to the management of a development project in an African culture.

YAMAJAMBERE CASE STUDY:

PARTICIPATIVE DEVELOPMENT IN BURUNDI

This case allows participants to trace and discuss the process of participatory development in a "Social Action Plan" adapted to Burundian realities. The National Program for Promotion of Social and Eco-

---

[4]Created by Lynn Pebbles, Washington, DC, 1981.

nomic Awareness Among Women developed a program to retrain and deploy social workers working in the country's various community social centers in order to obtain the participation of the local population and of their various levels of leadership in the development process.

Half a day is needed for this exercise which is implemented according to distinct steps:

Step 1: Individuals read Part I of the case on their own (30-45 minutes).

Step 2: They meet in small groups and discuss their findings (60 minutes).

Step 3: A plenary session to share ideas, comments, reactions is conducted by the trainer (60 minutes).

Step 4: Part II of the case is distributed and discussed (30 minutes).

PART I: THE CASE[5]

Burundi: A Developing Country

Slightly smaller than Belgium, Burundi is a small landlocked country lying just south of the Equator in East Africa. It lies between Rwanda to the north, Zaire to the west, and Tanzania to the east and south. Except for a narrow coastal plain along Lake Tanganyika in the west and marshy lowlands in the north and east, the country is composed predominantly of hills (see Map, Figure 35).

Figure 35.

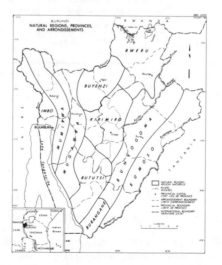

---

[5]This case study is based on an article written by P. Casse, and L. Magos, "L'Animation Sociale au Burundi," *International Review of Community Development,* No. 31-32, Summer 1974. It does not represent the views of the government of Burundi or of any organization.

The climate is equatorial with sufficient rainfall in most areas to support rainfed agriculture. A wide variety of agricultural commodities could be produced in quantity, including tea, cotton, quinquina, sugar, and livestock. Yet, little progress has been made in diversifying into crops other than traditional foodcrops and coffee, partially because of the physical isolation of the population and also because of widespread illiteracy and the consequent lack of awareness of the techniques and benefits of diversification.

Despite these obstacles, and as a result of the favorable climate and the dominant role of women's labor, the people have succeeded in establishing what amounts in quantitative terms, to a relatively acceptable food balance. Qualitatively there is a deficiency in fats and animal proteins in the diet of the local population.

Burundi has an essentially agricultural economy relying on subsistence farming and one principal export crop, coffee. Agriculture dominates Burundi's economy and constitutes 58% of the GNP, of which only 8% represents cash crops, the remainder being subsistence production. Yet agricultural productivity is low, because of the absence of modern inputs and the low skill level of the population at large. The land-locked position of the country makes transport to export markets long and costly.

Burundi was launched into independence in a state of extreme poverty. It faced a formidable set of disadvantages. Its natural resources were very limited and peat, kaolin, lime, etc. extremely difficult to process. Over 80 percent of its foreign exchange earnings depended on a single crop (coffee) which was subject to wide fluctuations not only in price but also in yield.

Per capita income was US$54. in 1970, of which only US$20. represents cash earnings, the balance being in the form of subsistence production. Burundi was included in the twenty-five countries defined by UNCTAD (1972, Santiago, Chile) as being the least developed in the world.

In Burundi, there are two principal ethnic groups, the Tutsis and the Hutus, of different historic-geographic origins, who, in spite of centuries of living together, have maintained separate sets of socio-cultural values. An upheaval in 1972 caused high migration and a temporarily reduced population growth rate. Now, however, it appears that the country may look ahead to a period of internal stability and the population is expected to grow at about 2.5% per annum again. This will cause increasing pressure on the land in a country where population density is already relatively high (142 per km^2).

At present, children below 20 years of age constitute 55% of the population. The age pyramid indicates substantial depletion of the male population above 20 years of age, primarily because of emigration, since typically it is an active male member of the family who migrates. Consequently, young women must often accept the lowest paying jobs in the economy.

The majority of the labor force is engaged in smallholder agriculture; opportunities for wage employment are extremely limited. Out of a total labor force of 1.9 million, only 6% are wage earners. Technicians and managers are predominantly European.

Of the country's 4.1 million population (in 1979), about 96% live in the rural areas on "rugos" (small, self-contained homesteads) on their own plot of land, instead of being grouped into small villages. Plots of arable land are scattered over the surrounding hillsides. Several "rugos" form each hillside community. Hillside communities are organized in communes.

The widely scattered population is a serious obstacle to the country's economic development. The official establishment of agricultural settlements in underpopulated areas on the plains and in the eastern part of the country would help to reduce excessive population densities in the other regions. The Government of Burundi is seeking to do this with United Nations support. It is encountering strong resistance, however, since the local inhabitants are deeply attached to their traditional homes on the mountains and are unwilling to leave these for regions which they consider alien.

The most immediate constraint on development is the lack of capacity to prepare and manage projects. There is an obvious need to expand training to make up for the lack of skilled manpower. But given the relative shortage of government finance, there is little hope for expanding expenditure on education. Attention must, therefore, be directed towards increasing the efficiency of the system within the existing financial allocations.

Only about 21% of the children of age to attend primary schools do so. The task facing the Government in the expansion of primary education is enormous. Education is dominated by many Catholic schools which have programs that are ill-adapted to the country's needs, producing an elite class very frequently cut off by the nature of its training from the rural sector and unsuited to respond to the country's economic needs. Appreciating these weaknesses, the Government embarked on the preparation of a reform in 1973. Burundi is trying to devise new programs relevant to the largely rural population. Secondary education will be restructured. Plans for the expansion of technical and vocational training are based on projections of the needs for skilled manpower. Some manpower planning is required to ensure that the numbers being trained in specific fields are geared to meet projected demand. It is in this context of reform that the "Program of Social Awareness" was born.

The Birth of a Program of Social Awareness

The project entitled "National Program for Promotion of Social and Economic Awareness Among Women" was the result of the efforts of a team that brought together, for a period of four years (1966-1969), a group of local and international experts and technicians. They had been asked by the Ministries of Social Affairs and Labor to prepare and introduce a "Social Action Plan" adapted to Burundian realities. Primary responsibility for the project rested with the Ministries of Social Affairs and of Labor and the Middle Classes which, by December 1965, had requested the Gitega Development Cooperation Center (Training Center for Supervisory Personnel, established on the basis of a special agreement signed by Belgium and Burundi in 1963) to prepare a program to retrain and deploy social workers presently working in the country's various community social centers.

A series of working meetings organized by the Center, with the active participation of the Ministry of Social Affairs, its Director General, the Director of Social Services and the Directorate of Community Social Centers led to the preparation of a project to retrain all women directors of the social centers and women instructors. A preliminary survey (December 1965 - March 1966) together with a pilot experiment in retraining (organized between March 12 and April 2, 1966) at the Gitega Development Cooperation Center paved the way for two appraisal reports that indicated to the authorities the need to expand the initial retraining project and convert this into a national program. The essential characteristic of this program was that it proposed, in conjunction with the training of all community development workers, structural and program reforms both in training and community development work. The draft program recommended a complete reorganization of the existing social service administrative machinery.

"Yamajambere" (To have more, To become better, To be more) was the motto expressing the global target of the National Program which was developed to obtain the cooperation and participation of the local population and of their various levels of leadership in the development process.

This goal opened up a number of options, the choice of which was determined on the basis of existing Burundian social and administrative realities. To what goals should efforts be directed? How can these objectives be best achieved? What methods should be used to enlist local participation? Who should participate in the action program?

The main initial effort during the first phase of the National Program was focused on the female rural population. This choice was made because, in the rural sector, women are considered to be the guardians of the traditional hierarchical structure. Modification of this role was a priority that had been indicated by other studies (specifically concerning the woman's role in such spheres as child training, farm production, organization of family life, health care, diet, etc.).

The main focus of this program was the old network of community social centers. Instead of training young girls in need of work, the centers were to be used to direct the attention of the new generation of adult women to their specific everyday problems. It would also help them in practical ways to deal more effectively with their needs, given the limitation of the national resources. The centers would thus make possible achievements in desired areas of progress.

The cornerstone of the Program was to be community participation, secured through the methods of social sensitization, community development and leadership training developed by IRAM (Institute for the Study and Application of Development Methods, Paris) and adapted to the socio-cultural conditions existing in Burundi.

The principle underlying the program is that methods of progress cannot be imposed or chosen by persons or agencies outside the local environment concerned, but that decisions of this type rest with the future beneficiaries of such programs. As R. Colin, the French Sociologist, has said, "At all levels, individuals are entitled to direct their own destiny."

In general, these methods of development of social awareness lead to the birth and strengthening of a true process of social self-help that extends to join up with the complementary but essential formal training effort.

The Development of Social Awareness in Agents of the Program

The retraining of the agents of the Program to assume future responsibility for local social awareness programs commenced in 1966 at the Development Cooperation Center. The timetable provided for two complete annual cycles of social awareness training from 1966 onwards with 20 women instructors participating in each cycle.[6] On this basis it

---

[6]In 1966 some 50 women instructors were employed either in the Ministry of Social Affairs in Bujumbura or in the community social centers. Holding diplomas from the schools of domestic economy (two to three years of post-primary studies) these women instructors were assisted by staff trained on the job in the community social centers.

was hoped that by 1971 a service with 160 women social facilitators (20 per province) would have been brought into being.[7]

Each eight-month training course was divided into three stages: 1) a three-month stage devoted to heightening the facilitator's own awareness of community problems and community development methods; 2) a four-month stage devoted to practical social sensitization and extension work; and 3) a one-month review stage.

1. Background training

The purpose of this stage was to develop a four-fold heightening of awareness in participating women instructors:

a. An awareness of the actual situation existing in local conditions in such priority areas as health, education, nutrition, farm problems, domestic economy and awareness of available local resources.

b. An awareness of the theoretical ideal, i.e., what conditions would be desirable to the local population.

c. An awareness of the obstacles and difficulties (material, psychological, socio-cultural) presently obstructing achievement of ideal conditions.

d. An awareness of how practical and possible it will be (in light of existing resources and constraints) to surmount the obstacles and make specific improvements in the existing conditions.

Curriculum for Background Training

— Social sensitization: theory and practice

— Teamwork methods

— Aspects of Development in Burundi

— Social Services: theory and practice

— Training and social progress

— Health problems

— Nutrition problems

— Problems of the domestic economy

— Problems of farm economics

— Clerical support and statistics

— Elements of agricultural extension work

— Social Workshops: their organization

All subjects in the curriculum were presented by experts or technicians using a standard technique of instruction, i.e., training by means of sensitization (heightening of awareness, consciousness-raising). This sensitization was introduced in four steps:

---

[7]Various factors made it impossible to follow the timetable set. By 1969 only 60 or so of these female instructors had been retrained.

Step 1: Course participants were asked by the instructor to discuss what they knew of existing problems and conditions (in nutrition, health, etc.) in the district that they were to work in.[8] If necessary, field visits were organized to obtain a better idea of such conditions and problems. (What is the actual situation?)

Step 2: The course instructor then described and explained the new developments in science and technology that could be applied in order to improve the existing situation. (What would bring about a better situation?)

Step 3: The instructor elicited comments concerning obstacles and difficulties which would prevent the existing situation from being improved. ("What you said is interesting but we could not do it here because…")

Step 4: The instructor organized a group from the participants into a team in order to find realistic, possible solutions to the problem at hand. (What can be done despite the obstacles and constraints?)

Women instructors were also trained in the techniques of social sensitization of the local rural population. The principal claim to originality of the instructional method adopted was that it enables the future social facilitators to experience the techniques that they themselves would soon be applying afterwards in the field.

Figure 36. Parallels Between the Background Course in Sensitization (or heightening of awareness) and the Role of Social Facilitators in the Rural Sector

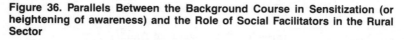

Course instructors		Social facilitator
Sensitization ———	Identification ———	Sensitization
	Heightened awareness of:	
	(1) existing conditions	
	(2) the ideal situation	
	(3) obstacles and constraints	
	(4) practical solutions	
Social facilitators		Rural population

---

[8]These courses were organized on a geographical basis; each cycle comprised in chronological order, female instructors from Gitega, Ngozi, Muyinga, Ruyigi, Bujumbura, Muramuya, and Bubanza in Burundi.

2. Practical Training

Over a four-month period course participants (in groups of two) are required to field-test applications of their background training gained during the sensitization stage. They were asked: to verify whether classroom analysis of problems had been pertinent; to try out training techniques learned; and to attempt any necessary improvements.

3. Review

The review or final stage in the training process was designed to draw conclusions from field experience and compare theoretical knowledge with practice.

As a final exercise participants and instructors worked together on the preparation of a sensitization program. A working instrument was thereby created to assist facilitators with the launching of social awareness training in the rural sector.

Reform of the Structures and Mechanisms of Social Action

In the face of the failure of existing outdated training and community facilities, a reorganization of social action mechanisms was clearly necessary. In 1966 Burundi possessed 53 community social centers located as follows:

Province	No. of community social centers	Province	No. of community social centers
Gitega	6	Ruyigi	4
Ngozi	13	Muramuya	4
Bujumbura	10	Bubanza	4
Muyinga	2	Bururi	10

The government community social centers constituted a minority of these and of subsidized community social centers, formed and managed by the various religious groups, which were all answerable to the Department of Community Social Centers (Ministry of Social Affairs). Generally speaking, the community social centers, with the exception perhaps of those in Gitega and Bujumbura, were in an unsatisfactory condition. Most of them had been left completely isolated because the authorities responsible for community social centers were completely without resources. The main criticisms that could be leveled at the system in existence in 1966 are summarized below:

— Programs completely unrelated to the real needs of the people

— Detachment of the community social center from the surrounding population groups (practically no adults visited the community center)

The reform consisted of: 1) the creation of a steering and technical committee for social action; 2) the establishment of regional training headquarters; 3) the definition of a new role for community social centers; and 4) the setting up of social extension posts.

The Steering and Technical Committee for Social Action

The role of the committee (directly answerable to the Minister of Social Affairs) was to promote and implement social action programs at the national level. Government officials, experts, technicians, and religious authorities would thus be brought together into a single body. The Committee would also be primarily responsible for advising the Minister on social and cultural questions of any kind that arose out of development plans.

Another reason for the committee's existence was to strengthen the machinery for coordinating all programs for social enhancement in Burundi.

Bodies Engaged in Social Promotion Programs in 1966

UPRONA (national party)	National training effort; community development work
JRR (youth organization)	Promotion of social awareness in young people
UFB (Union of Burundian Women)	Promotion of social awareness in rural and urban sectors
Ministry of Agriculture	Nyabumira Rural Training Center, agricultural extension services
AIDR (International Association for Rural Development)	Promotion of social awareness in the combined Karuzi-Ruyigi development area (sensitization training in the rural sector; sensitization training for women).
CERAS (Center for Research and Social Promotion)	Social promotion within the Catholic Church

WHO (World Health Organization)	Health and nutrition training (Health Centers)
FAO (Food and Agriculture Organization of the U.N.)	Promotion of social awareness in the rural sector (Rural radio project)

Regional Training Headquarters

Responsible for social promotion throughout a given region, the regional training headquarters (also known as the provincial community social center) was to act as an intermediary between community social centers and the department supervising them; to organize training seminars for women social facilitators working in the province; and to provide logistical support (material and technical) for the staff of the social extension posts. It was also set up to practice demonstrations for trainee facilitators.

To perform this regional training function effectively the regional training headquarters should have a mobile equipment unit, a mobile multidisciplinary technical team, and office support staff.[9]

A New Role for Community Social Centers

In brief, the plan provided for a change in the function of community social centers. These centers were, on the one hand, to serve as social workshops (for production and sales) and, on the other, act as the prime movers in social sensitization retraining programs for all local technical personnel and leaders (missionaries, teachers, health workers, veterinarians, etc.). In addition, these centers would be the headquarters for launching rural social sensitization and extension programs. The community social center would continue to act as a base for the activities of the social facilitators.

Social Extension Posts

The social extension posts were designed to respond to the real needs of the local rural population by helping them through various training programs, to initiate those development measures to which they attached the greatest priority.

At the national planning level, the social extension posts performed a vitally important role, providing an ideal mechanism for reconciling the desires of the population, while deferring to the real constraints and

---

[9]UNICEF had been approached as a possible source for part of the training equipment needed. An agreement was reached in 1968.

requirements of development planning. They also provided a communications point for information flows from the administrators to the rural population and from the rural population to the administrators. This exchange of ideas can be seen in the schematic representation of the organization of the mechanisms of social action on the following page (see Figure 37).

The National Program in Operation

Women social facilitators were entirely responsible for promotion of social self-help movements. In Burundi, the promotion of social self-help required four distinct steps. When the social workers returned to their respective community social centers from their sensitization training, they were required to make a survey and a series of contacts prior to launching social sensitization programs of their own, set up a rural social sensitization center and then introduce and go forward with the rural social sensitization program itself. These four steps would be achieved with the help of facilitators representing the hillside communities.

Step 1: Survey and Preliminary Contacts

The purpose of these surveys was to gather data pertinent to the promotion of social awareness. An indication of the kind of information the facilitators had to collect follows.

• Census of communes and districts within the area of influence of each community social center

• Census of hill communities by commune and by district

• Census of population makeup (men, women, children)

• Identification of government administrative officers and heads of district

• Inventory of possible logistic support points (dispensaries, missions, school buildings, etc.)

• Choice of site for the first social extension post

These preliminary contacts were designed to ensure that social facilitators received full cooperation of local authorities and of the local population.

Figure 37. Schematic Representation of the Organization of Mechanisms of Social Action

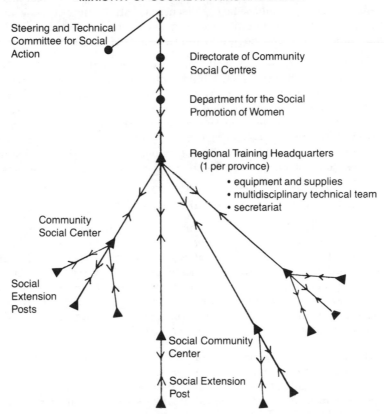

MINISTRY OF SOCIAL AFFAIRS AND LABOR

Steering and Technical
Committee for Social
Action

Directorate of Community
Social Centres

Department for the Social
Promotion of Women

Regional Training Headquarters
  (1 per province)
  • equipment and supplies
  • multidisciplinary technical team
  • secretariat

Community
Social Center

Social
Extension
Posts

Social Community
Center

Social Extension
Post

Facilitators were advised not to make their first approaches to government officials without the assistance of their regional training headquarters or authorities at the Ministry of Social Affairs. This was because it was considered that the regional training headquarters staff would be better able to arouse the interest of regional and local administrators which would be necessary to obtain the support of the provincial governors. Once the authorities were "pre-sensitized", the facilitators could then directly approach the local authorities and local persons of influence (the advisory council for the commune). It was assumed they would then meet with less resistance from local administrators. Assured of their support, they could then proceed to make contact with the people themselves.

The facilitators were required to explain the aims and methods of the social sensitization program to government and, in certain cases, religious officials. At this time, goals of the hillside communities could be defined; meetings could be held to discuss potential improvements; and then, the hillside communities, together with the local officials, could make plans for improvements within the limits of the possible.

To the local advisory councils and local representatives chosen by these councils, the facilitators would explain in simple terms the whys of the social sensitization program. ("These meetings of hillside communities have been called so that we can examine together our present condition, our aspirations and the obstacles in the way of *yamajambere* - progress and so that we can together see what improvements can be made in our living standards.") At this point, it would be possible to proceed to construct the first elements of a new mechanism for social action.

Step 2: Establishment of a Social Extension Post

Meetings with the local population were called to explain the nature of the social sensitization process. The social extension post was intended to serve as a meeting place between the community social center and the hillside rugos (homesteads). Often, whatever meeting place happened to be selected became the social extension post. It had to be a place easily recognizable (a crossroads, an old homestead, etc.) to the local population. Places no more than 45 minutes walking time for any person attending meetings were preferred.

At the same time the meeting place was being selected, the facilitators would ask the local women to choose delegates[10] to represent the hillside communities invited to participate actively in social sensitization meetings. At this stage, the assistance of the local advisory councils proved to be invaluable. The decisions on how often meetings were to be held (once a week at least) and on what day and at what time were made by the local women. Since only some women were able to attend the social sensitization meetings, and in order to ensure the widest possible dissemination of information, the facilitator would promise to hold a general meeting open to everyone once a month and to visit the individual hillside communities as often as possible.

When the national program was launched, only one extension post was set up serving some 10 or 12 hillside communities. Others were established later depending on the wishes of the local population and the availability of facilitators.

---

[10]As a general rule, two delegates representing the new community were selected to represent each hillside. It should be noted that UFB (Union of Burundian Women) was particularly effective in helping social facilitators in the selection of delegates.

Step 3: Work at the Social Extension Post

In the course of meeting representatives of the hillside communities at the extension post, each facilitator first sought to define as clearly as possible the aims of the social sensitization program:

> "...Our aim is to meet regularly in the hillside communities in order to consider together the problems that we face and our condition of life (health, children, culture, money, food, etc.), and to examine together what improvements can be made within the limits of our resources and local traditional roles."

The facilitator, whose own role was "non-directive", could seek to clearly define, in association with the elected delegates, their responsibility for disseminating information among the women of their immediate community; report the community's conclusions, ideas, and feelings; and describe work done by the community as a group.

Adopting the methods learned in the course of training in the field as part of the social sensitization program, they would then seek to increase the awareness of the more pressing problems voiced by the community's delegates:

• How do things stand now? (The women indicate how they are faring in relation to nutrition, the upbringing of children, etc.)

• Would it not be better if...? (The facilitator, with expert support if necessary, describes what could be done)

• What are the obstacles in the way of improving a given situation? (Noting the reactions of delegates who are skeptical and considering suggestions from other community delegates)

• Despite the obstacles, can we not change and improve the existing situation? (Possible practical solutions)

At the end of each meeting the delegates returned home and were asked to discuss with their own group the results of the various encounters they had attended. A monthly general meeting (open to the entire community) was organized at the extension post. During this meeting, delegates themselves reported on the results of the month's discussions and exchanged views.

Step 4: Social Self-Help in the Hillside Community Itself

It was hoped that a multiplier effect would result from delegates' activities in the communities, where information spread by word of mouth from household to household, family to family, or through meetings called as a result of action by influential community members.

The final result of the Program at the grassroots level was threefold:

(1) Communities decided upon the priorities to be given to their own needs,

(2) They organized themselves to respond to the priorities established (emergence of "social awareness networks", i.e., a development structure), and

(3) They engaged in projects with the help of the facilitator and technicians, who provided them with the tools (the apparatus of development) and the necessary instruction (the apparatus of technical assistance).

Gradually they developed an interchange of information between the facilitators/technicians and the local community that led to valuable insights and imposed a sense of "community effort and solidarity on development work." We define such development as *development by objectives*.

Questions and Issues

1. What are the main cultural aspects of the development project described?

2. How was the participative process managed

   (a) before the *Yamajabere* program started?
   (b) after its inception?

3. What is your evaluation of the training program designed for the social workers?

4. What questions would you ask to the people who have been involved in the design and implementation of this program?

5. Do you recognize some of the four value orientations?

PART II

Comments by someone who participated in the design and implementation of the project.

We are quite reluctant to regard participation as a panacea. It is merely one method of development which has both merits and disadvantages.

Our experience in Burundi led us to consider five factors as essential to the successful organization of a social awareness and sensitization program:

1. Above all else, responsibility in the choice of development objectives, instruments, and actions, whether local, regional, or national, *must be shared* between the authorities and their representatives (offi-

cials, religious groups, etc.) and technical professionals (experts, technicians, etc.) on one hand and the local population on the other.

2. It is desirable to use the services of specialized technicians and social service workers in the mechanisms of social action (communication, teamwork, information transfer, extension, sensitization, resistance to change, etc.).

3. Social organizers and facilitators should respect the local traditions and customs in the community and not attempt manipulations that invariably encounter resistance.

4. Recognition that socio-political structures may need to be adapted *in situ* to ensure maximum results from the techniques of social sensitization.

5. If social facilitation and extension work is to be conducted under the best conditions, permanent logistic support (administrative, technical, and procurement assistance) is essential.

In analyzing the social sensitization program organized in Burundi, we must acknowledge that two factors have unfortunately been absent, i.e.,

a) A clear political determination to apply the social sensitization process, involving the participation of the elements of leadership and of the local population in the development program;

b) The organization of effective logistic support in order to consolidate, strengthen, and augment the actions of social facilitators which are presently scattered ineffectively throughout the country.

The reaction of the rural population to the program was generally very positive. Some obstacles were, however, apparent at different stages in the implementation of the program: for example, 1) the women's belief that the sensitization process would provide them with some drugs, seeds, and other material things; 2) difficulties over the arrangement of meetings as a result of the dispersal of communities; 3) the reluctance of some women to choose delegates (due to the sense of family being more highly developed than the community spirit); and 4) the expectation of the rural population to regard the facilitator as a counselor with all the answers.

The support of the local government officials varied from one region to another.

To sum up, then, we could not but praise the work of these social workers who, although often isolated and lacking technical support, achieved a remarkable performance. In 1982, 15 years after it was launched, the Program still continues despite limitations. Its longevity and persistence must certainly be attributed to the energy and determination of the social facilitators who have continued to build an evolving society on a basis of dialogue and social self-help.

Exercise H. The following checklist on *"participative management of people"* is distributed to the participants who answer the questions, determine the profile of their own organizations and discuss it in small groups.

Figure 38. A Checklist on the Participative Management of People[11]

Please put a check on each scale taking into account your perception of the overall situation in your unit or organization.

Managerial Indicators

Personal Assessment

Managerial Indicators	0	1	2	3	4	5
1. How do you assess the overall management of people?	Non-satisfactory		Satisfactory			Excellent
2. Do managers care for people?	Not at all		Fairly so			Very much so
3. How often are your skills used?	Under used		Well used			Fully used
4. What kind of opportunity to grow on the job do you have?	Nil		Fair			Very good
5. How do you perceive the coordination of efforts within the organization?	Insufficient		Sufficient but could be improved			Sufficient & very effective

---

[11]This checklist has been created using the information presented in the booklet on "Managing People in the World Bank Group. Guidelines for Managers," World Bank (Washington, DC, February 1981).

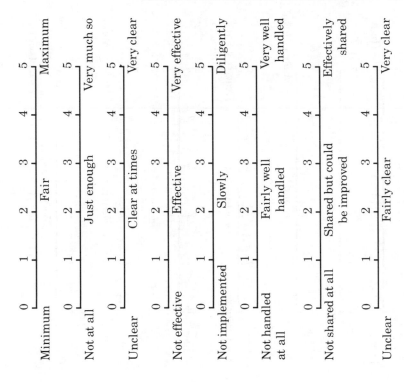

6. How do you assess your freedom to speak up when discussing work-related issues?

0	1	2	3	4	5
Minimum		Fair			Maximum

7. To what extent do the managers delegate responsibility?

0	1	2	3	4	5
Not at all		Just enough			Very much so

8. How clear is the managers' position regarding policy issues?

0	1	2	3	4	5
Unclear		Clear at times			Very clear

9. How do you assess the decision-making process within the organization?

0	1	2	3	4	5
Not effective		Effective			Very effective

10. How well are decisions implemented?

0	1	2	3	4	5
Not implemented		Slowly			Diligently

11. How is change handled within the organization?

0	1	2	3	4	5
Not handled at all		Fairly well handled			Very well handled

12. How well is information shared in the organization?

0	1	2	3	4	5
Not shared at all		Shared but could be improved			Effectively shared

13. How clear are the organization objectives and priorities?

0	1	2	3	4	5
Unclear		Fairly clear			Very clear

14. How do you assess your own commitment regarding the organization program?

0	1	2	3	4	5
Low			Medium		High

15. How innovative is the organization?

0	1	2	3	4	5
Not at all			Moderately so		Very much so

16. How do you perceive the breakdown of working responsibility within the organization?

0	1	2	3	4	5
Does not make sense			Could be improved		Makes a lot of sense

17. How do you assess the support you get from the managers?

0	1	2	3	4	5
Not enough			Just enough		Exactly what's needed

18. How is cooperation in the organization?

0	1	2	3	4	5
Does not exist			Exists but could be improved		Very effective

19. How does your job relate to others within the organization?

0	1	2	3	4	5
Isolated			Moderately integrated		Well integrated

20. According to you, how motivated are the employees?

0	1	2	3	4	5
Not at all			Moderately motivated		Highly motivated

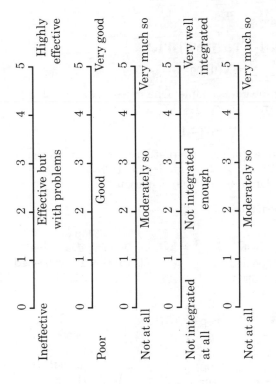

21. How do you assess the organization's performance appraisal system?

0	1	2	3	4	5
Ineffective		Effective but with problems			Highly effective

22. How do you assess the leadership in the organization?

0	1	2	3	4	5
Poor		Good			Very good

23. How concerned are managers with employee development and training?

0	1	2	3	4	5
Not at all		Moderately so			Very much so

24. How would you assess the integration of various units in the organization?

0	1	2	3	4	5
Not integrated at all		Not integrated enough			Very well integrated

25. How interested are you in pursuing this survey on management?

0	1	2	3	4	5
Not at all		Moderately so			Very much so

5. Time: Two days

6. Conceptual Framework:

INPUT 1-A

The solution to the problem is simple: One must make sure that A gets into the station first.

INPUT 1-B

If the development process of a given situation can be described as an operation in six steps (Figure 39. The Development Process), then one can also pinpoint six different types of participation.

Figure 39. The Development Process

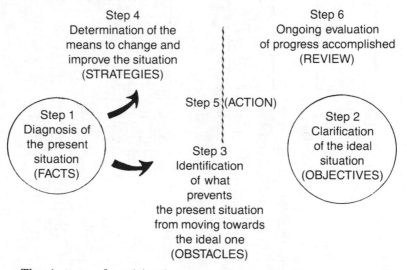

The six types of participation are:

1. Participation in the diagnosis of the present situation (What or who are we? Positive and negative aspects of the present and actual situation?).

2. Participation in the selection of objectives (What do we want? What are our goals? What is the ideal situation for us?).

3. Participation in the identification of the obstacles which prevent the situation from improving naturally, easily (What are the internal and external obstacles?).

4. Participation in the decision-making process regarding the choice of strategies (How are we to change the status quo? Action plan?).

5. Participation in the action itself (doing).

6. Participation in the ongoing review of the progress accomplished (Where are we? How are we doing? What do we have to adjust?).

INPUT 2

The development/management process in an organization or a society can be defined in terms of the reduction of the tension which exists between decision-makers and people (community members, team members, farmers, employees, workers...) through communication, empathy and *participation*.

The problem

In many cases a gap exists between the decision-makers perception regarding the development/management process and the people's expectations. (Figure 40.)

Figure 40. The Political Dialectic of Development/Management

DECISION-MAKERS
(Administrators, Managers, Professionals, Politicians...)

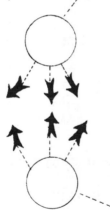

Development and management are perceived in terms of:

A. Development/management goals
B. Directions for progress

B. Selection of priorities
A. Expression of needs (including *BASIC* needs)

PEOPLE
(Managers, Farmers, Employees...)

The tension between decision-makers and people can be established as follows:

1. People express needs and preferences (see workshop on motivation).

2. Decision-makers' perceptions of development are more in line with the setting of goals, the identification of resources available as well as the constraints to be considered.

3. If the gap between the directions for development/management as determined by the "elite" and the needs as perceived, felt and expressed by the people is too big, a *"block"* results.

4. From the "block" which is due to the contradiction between what progress should be according to the decision-makers and the people's wishes, two reactions derive:

"The elite" managers, because they do not get the expected reactions from the people (managers), start to complain about their apathy, indifference, irresponsibility and passivity.

People (managers), because they believe that no one is making any effort to meet their needs, criticize the "elite" (managers) for their lack of care, ineffectiveness and arrogance.

In most cases, the tension between the two partners, the managers/employees, creates an unhealthy situation. Value judgments are passed upon other groups; scapegoats appear; hostility develops; and last but not least, a fundamental contradiction surfaces in the social system organization, which can sometimes lead to an explosive situation (i.e. a revolution).

The solution

The solution is obvious. A *bridge* must be built between those who make decisions and the people. (Figure 41)

Figure 41. The Participatory or Bridging Process

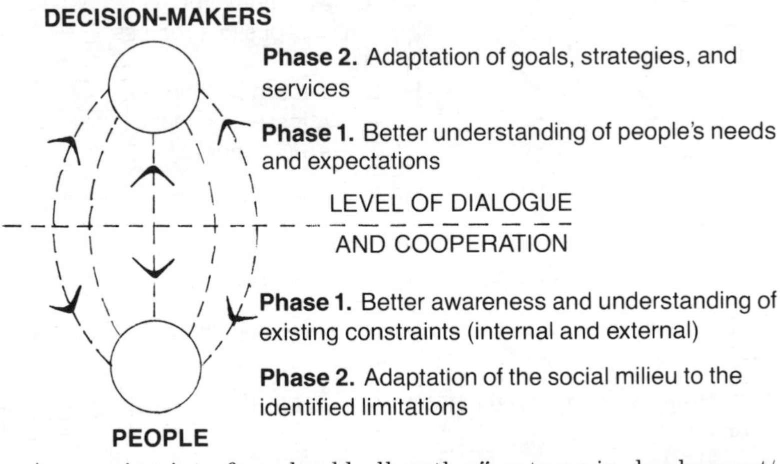

DECISION-MAKERS

Phase 2. Adaptation of goals, strategies, and services

Phase 1. Better understanding of people's needs and expectations

LEVEL OF DIALOGUE

AND COOPERATION

Phase 1. Better awareness and understanding of existing constraints (internal and external)

Phase 2. Adaptation of the social milieu to the identified limitations

PEOPLE

An ongoing interface should allow the "partners in development/management" to improve their reciprocal understanding and agree upon some form of joint action.

The process goes like this: through the interaction with people, decision-makers become more aware of and sensitive (Phase 1) about (a) the needs and expectations of the people concerned; (b) the psychological, economic, physical and cultural constraints which exist in the social system; and (c) the potential of the people. Knowing more about the social reality they have been separated from, the decision-makers are now better armed to adapt (Phase 2) their goals, strategies, services and support to the people so that they are able to maximize their lives and developments.

At the same time, the people (Phase 1) realize better what the technical, financial, physical and other constraints, which prevent the accomplishment of their wishes, are and they also improve their understanding of what the decision-makers try to achieve.

Finally, they learn more about the services available and how to use them. Building on their new awareness, they become more open to reconsidering (Phase 2) their needs, expectations in view of the existing limitations. They are also better informed of the cost involved in achieving their goals.

7. Handouts and Readings:

(a) Handouts

Bourdon, R.D., "A Basic Model for Employee Participation," *Training and Development Journal,* April 1980.

Brown, D.S., "Notifying Bureaucratic Systems in the Developing World," *Asian Forum,* Vol. VI, No. 1, January-March 1974, pp. 3-18.

Casse, P., "La Participation Sociétale au Développement: Rouages et Mechanismes," *Afrique,* Vol. XI, No. 2, 1972.

Chambers, P., "Do-it-Yourself Management Development," *International Management,* October 1974, pp. 46-50.

Colin, R., "L'Animation, Clé de Boute du Développement," *Développement et Civilisations,* 21 March 1965, pp. 5-9.

Connor, D.M., "Constructive Citizen Participation," *The 1977 Annual Handbook for Group Facilitators,* pp. 209-216.

Gepson, J., Martinko, M.J., and Belina, J., "Nominal Group Techniques," *Training and Development Journal,* September 1981.

Harrison, R., "Developing Autonomy, Initiative and Risk-Taking Through a Laboratory Design," *European Training,* Vol. 2, No. 2, pp. 101-116.

Hersey, P., and Blanchard, K.H., "The Management of Change," *Training and Development Journal*, June 1980.

Melman, S., "Industrial Efficiency Under Managerial -vs- Cooperative Decision-Making," *Review of Radical Political Economics*, Spring 1970, p. 18.

Moran, R.T., "Japanese Participative Management—or How Sinji Seido Can Work For You," *Advanced Management Journal*, Summer 1979.

Obradovic, J., "Participation and Work Attitudes in Yugoslavia," *Industrial Relations*, IX, February 1970, pp. 161-169.

Scott, D., and Deadrick, D., "The Nominal Group Technique: Applications for Training Needs Assessment," *Training and Development Journal*, June 1982.

Yager, E., "Quality Circle: A Tool for the '80s," *Training and Development Journal*, August 1980.

(b) Readings

Adizes, I., and Borgese, E.M. (eds.), *Self-Management: New Dimensions to Democracy*. Santa Barbara: Clio Press, 1975.

Batten, T.A., *Communities and Their Development*. London: Oxford University Press, 1957.

Benedict, D., *Worker Participation in Decision-Making in Industry: Forms, Experiences and Attitudes*. McMaster University, Reference Paper No. 78-01, 1977.

Berger, P.L., *Pyramids of Sacrifice (Political Ethics and Social Change)*. New York: Anchor Books, 1976.

Bernstein, P., *Workplace Democratization: It's Internal Dynamics*. Kent State: Kent State University Press, 1976.

Biddle, W.W., and Louriede, J.B., *The Community Development Process*. New York: Holt, Rinehart and Winston, 1965.

Clegg, H.A., *A New Approach to Industrial Democracy*. Oxford: Basil Blackwell, 1963.

Dickson, P., *The Future of the Workplace*. New York: Weybright and Talley, 1975.

Espinosa, J.G., and Zimbaust, A.S., *Economic Democracy: Workers' Participation in Chilean Industry, 1970-1973*. New York: Academic Press, 1978.

Freire, Paolo, *Pedagogy of the Oppressed*. New York: Seabury Press, 1973.

Gardner, J.W., *Self-Renewal*. New York: Harper and Row, 1963.

Goodenough, W.H., *Cooperation in Change*. New York: Russel Sage Foundation, 1963.

Gyllenhammar, P.G., *People at Work*. New York: Addison-Wesley, 1977.

Horvat, B., Markovic, M., Supek, R. (eds.), *Self-Governing Socialism, Vols. I and II*. White Plains: International Arts and Sciences Press, 1975.

Kilaja, J., *Worker's Councils: The Yugoslav Experience*. New York: Frederick A. Praeger, 1966.

Knight, P., "Peru's Social Poverty Sector: Development Through December 1975 and Projects for Expansion." World Bank, 1976.

Lebret, L.J., *Dynamique Concrète du Développement*. Paris: Les Editions Ouvrières, 1961.

Meister, A., *La Participation pour le Développement*. Paris: Les Editions Ouvrières, 1977.

O'Toole, J., *Work and the Quality of Life*. Cambridge: MIT Press, 1974.

Pateman, C., *Participation and Democratic Theory*. Cambridge: University Press, 1973.

Pye, L.W. (ed.), *Communications and Political Development*. Princeton, NJ: Princeton University Press, 1972.

Vaner, J., *The Economics of Workers' Management: A Yugoslav Case Study*. London: George Adlen and Unurin Ltd., 1972.

Reading List

A list of twelve books to read:

Bateson, G., *Mind and Nature: A Necessary Unity.* New York: Bantam Books, 1979.

Berger, P.L., *Pyramids of Sacrifice.* New York: Anchor Books, 1976.

Drucker, P.F., *Management: Tasks, Responsibilities, Practices.* New York: Harper and Row, 1974.

French, W.L., and Bell, C.H., *Organization Development: Behavioral Sciences Interventions for Organization Improvement.* Englewood Cliffs, NJ: Prentice-Hall, Inc., 1973.

Hersey, P., and Blanchard, K.H., *Management of Organizational Behavior.* Englewood Cliffs, NJ: Prentice-Hall Inc., 1977.

Jay A., *Cooperation Man.* New York: Pocket Books, 1973.

Jones, D.C., and Svejnar, J., *Participatory and Self-Managed Firms.* Lexington, Mass: Lexington Books, 1982.

Koontz, H., and O'Donnell, C., *Essentials of Management.* New York: McGraw-Hill Book Company, 1974.

Maccoby, M., *The Gamesman: The New Corporate Leaders.* New York: Simon and Schuster, 1976.

Moran, R.T., and Harris, P.R., *Managing Cultural Differences.* Houston: Gulf Publishing Company, 1979.

Stewart, E.C., *American Cultural Patterns.* Chicago: Intercultural Press, 1977.

Uphoff, N.T., Cohen, J.M., and Goldsmith, A.A., *Feasibility and Application of Mind Development Participation: A State-of-the-Art Paper.* New York: Cornell University, 1979.

Postscript

"For years I have truly tried to live in accordance with your teachings," I said. "Obviously I have not done well. How can I do better now?"

"You think and talk too much. You must stop talking to yourself."

"What do you mean?"

"You talk to yourself too much. You're not unique in that. Every one of us does that. We carry on an internal talk. Think about it. Whenever you are alone, what do you do?"

"I talk to myself."

"What do you talk to yourself about?"

"I don't know; anything, I suppose."

"I'll tell you what we talk to ourselves about. We talk about the world. In fact we maintain our world with our internal talk."

"How do we do that?"

"Whenever we finish talking to ourselves the world is always as it should be. We renew it, we kindle it with life, we uphold it with our internal talk. Not only that, but we also choose our paths as we talk to ourselves. Thus we repeat the same choices over and over until the day we die, because we keep on repeating the same internal talk over and over until the day we die. A warrior is aware of this and strives to stop his talking. This is the last point you have to know if you want to live like a warrior."

"How can I stop talking to myself?"

"First of all you must use your ears to take some of the burden from your eyes. We have been using our eyes to judge the world since the time we were bore. We talk to others and to ourselves mainly about what we see. A warrior is aware of that and listens to the world; he listens to the sounds of the world."[1]

Carlos Castaneda
A Separate Reality

---

[1]Carlos Castaneda, *A Separate Reality* (New York: Pocket Books, 1972), pp. 262-263.